Helion & Company Limited
Unit 8 Amherst Business Centre
Budbrooke Road
Warwick
CV34 5WE
England
Tel. 01926 499 619
Fax 0121 711 4075
Email: info@helion.co.uk
Website: www.helion.co.uk
Twitter: @helionbooks
Visit our blog http://blog.helion.co.uk/

Published by Helion & Company 2018
Designed and typeset by Mach 3 Solutions
Ltd (www.mach3solutions.co.uk)
Cover designed by Paul Hewitt, Battlefield
Design (www.battlefield-design.co.uk)
Printed by Henry Ling Limited, Dorchester,
Dorset

Text © Adrien Fontanellaz and
Tom Cooper 2018
Maps drawn by and © Tom Cooper 2018
Photographs © as individually credited
Colour profiles © Tom Cooper /
David Bocquelet 2017, as indicated

ISBN 978-1-912390-30-4

British Library Cataloguing-in-Publication
Data.
A catalogue record for this book is available
from the British Library.

For details of other military history titles
published by Helion & Company
Limited contact the above address, or visit
our website: http://www.helion.co.uk.

We always welcome receiving book
proposals from prospective authors.

CONTENTS

CW00816399

Cover Image

This pair of Ethiopian T-54/T-55s was knocked out by the EPLF during the bitter fighting on the streets of Massawa in February 1990. (Photo by Dan Connell)

Acknowledgments

This book is the result of cooperation with a number of individuals from the Horn of Africa, who generously helped with background and insider knowledge, and relevant information and expertise, foremost the late Major-General Ashenafi Gebre Tsadik (EtAF ret.) and Colonel Berhanu Wubneh (EtAF ret.). While establishing contact with them and prompting them to share their recollections proved a very complex and problematic task, there is little doubt that it would have been impossible to realize this project without their kind help and patience. Not a few others have initially refused any kind of contact, but eventually agreed to grant verbal or written narratives solely on condition of absolute anonymity – for reasons of concerns for their own, and the safety of their families. We would like to express our special gratitude to everybody involved, but also to promise to keep the memory of a number of persons that have passed away in the meantime, or those that are in poor health now.

Fortunately, Ethiopian military history has been extensively studied by native academic researchers, who produced several seminal works, based on documentation from official archives. In particular, works by Fantahun Ayele and Gebru Tareke provide a host of detail about military operations in Ethiopia of the 1980s.

We would also like to thank to Dan Connell, who has made numerous journeys to Eritrea since the 1970s, and published several books about his experiences and kindly allowed us to use his pictures, and to Paulos Asfaha, from Switzerland, for sharing his extensive knowledge of modern Ethiopian and Eritrean history. Last but not least, we would like to express our gratitude to Albert Grandolini and Jacques Guillem from France; Pit Weinert from Germany; Claudio Toselli and Roberto Gentilli from Italy; Jeroen Nijmeijer from The Netherlands; Mark Lepko and Tom Long from the USA for providing extensive aid in photographic, and other forms of research that, eventually, made this book possible.

Abbreviations

AB	Air Base	**FRA**	First Revolutionary Army (Ethiopian Army)
ADU	Afar Democratic Union	**FORA**	Fourth Revolutionary Army (Ethiopian Army)
An	Antonov (the design bureau led by Oleg Antonov)	**GPDF**	Gambela People's Democratic Front
APC	Armoured Personnel Carrier	**IAP**	International Airport
ASCC	Air Standardisation Coordinating Committee (of the NATO)	**ICRC**	International Committee of the Red Cross
		IEA	Imperial Ethiopian Aviation
BPLF	Bani Shangul People's Liberation Front	**IEAF**	Imperial Ethiopian Air Force
CAP	combat air patrol	**IEAA**	Imperial Ethiopian Army Aviation
CAS	close air support	**IFV**	Infantry fighting vehicle
CBU	cluster bomb unit	**IR**	Infra-red, electromagnetic radiation longer than deepest red light sensed as heat
C-in-C	Commander-in-Chief		
CO	Commanding Officer	**Il**	Ilyushin (the design bureau led by Sergey Vladimirovich Ilyushin, also known as OKB-39)
COIN	counterinsurgency		
EAL	Ethiopian Airlines	**MANPAD(S)**	man-portable air defence system(s) – light surface-to-air missile system that can be carried and deployed in combat by a single soldier
EDORM	Ethiopian Democratic Officers' Revolutionary Movement		
		MBT	Main Battle Tank
ELA	Eritrean Liberation Army	**Mi**	Mil (Soviet/Russian helicopter designer and manufacturer)
ELF	Eritrean Liberation Front		
ELINT	Electronic intelligence	**MIA**	missing in action
EPDM	Ethiopian People's Democratic Movement	**MiG**	Mikoyan i Gurevich (the design bureau led by Artyom Ivanovich Mikoyan and Mikhail Iosifovich Gurevich, also known as OKB-155 or MMZ' "Zenit")
EPLA	Eritrean People's Liberation Army (until 1993)		
EPLF	Eritrean People's Liberation Front (until 1993)		
EPRDF	Ethiopian People's Revolutionary Democratic Front		
EPRP	Eritrean People's Revolutionary Party		
ERA	Eritrean Relief Association	**MOND**	Ministry of National Defence (Ethiopia)
ERDF	Eritrean Defence Force (since 1993)	**MRLS**	multiple rocket launcher system
EtAF	Ethiopian Air Force	**OAU**	Organisation of African Unity

OLF	Oromo Liberation Front		RWR	Radar Warning Receiver
OPDO	Oromo People's Democratic Organisation		SAM	surface-to-air missile
PFDJ	People's Front for Democracy and Justice (Eritrea since 1993)		SMSC	Supreme Military Strategic Committee
			SPLA	Sudanese People's Liberation Army (Sudan)
PGE	Provisional Government of Eritrea		SRA	Second Revolutionary Army (Ethiopian Army)
PMAC	Provisional Military Administrative Committee (120-member committee of Ethiopian officers, better known as the 'Derg' or 'Dergue')		TPLA	Tigrayan People's Liberation Army
			TPLF	Tigrayan People's Liberation Front
			UN	United Nations
RAF	Royal Air Force		US$	United States Dollar
REST	Relief Society of Tigray		USSR	Union of Soviet Socialist Republics

Addenda to Africa@War 18: Wings over Ogaden, pp.49-50 & Africa@War 29: Ethiopian-Eritrean Wars, Volume 1, Eritrean Liberation War, 1961-1988, p.31

Since the publication of Volume 1 of this mini-series, the authors have managed to find further details on the Cuban military presence in Ethiopia in the 1977-1978 period. The precise identity of the units in question were the Tercera Brigada de Tanques and Décima Brigada de Tanques (3rd and 10th Armoured Brigades), Séptima Brigada de Infanteria Motorizada (7th Motorized Infantry Brigade), and the Quinta Brigade de Artilleria (5th Artillery Brigade). Operating equipment owned by Ethiopia, all of these units took part in the final battles of the Ogaden War, although not at their nominal full strength.

Addenda to Africa@War 29: Ethiopian-Eritrean Wars, Volume 1, Eritrean Liberation War, 1961-1988, p.51

The fighter-bomber of the Ethiopian air force shot down over Naqfa on 16 April 1984, was either a MiG-23BN or a MiG-23ML. It is certain that its pilot was Major Bezabih Petros – fresh back from a conversion course for MiG-23MLs at Lugovaya AB, in the former Soviet Union. Petros was to spend the next seven years as a prisoner of war in the hands of the Eritrean People's Liberation Front (EPLF).[1]

Alemayehu Essatu, Berhanu Wubneh, an unknown Angolan or Libyan pilot, Bezabih Petros (with cap and sun glasses), and Alemayehu Haile during the conversion course for MiG-23s, in Lugovaya, USSR, in 1983. (EtAF via S. N.)

Taken at Debre Zeit AB, this photograph shows MiG-21bis serial number 1091 with pilots (from left to right): Negussie Zergaw, Woldesellassie Tilahun, Bezabih Petros, Taile Bekele and Taile Aweke. (EtAF via S. N.)

CHAPTER 1
INTRODUCTION

For much of the 1980s, reports had been released by the Western media about a little known, yet particularly bitter war on the African Horn. Often combined with news about a terrible drought and famine, these indicated an uprising in north-eastern Ethiopia against what at the time was perceived as a 'Soviet-supported regime' in Addis Ababa. On its own, this was 'nothing new', because reports about local uprisings, military coups and other kind of political unrest in Ethiopia were quite frequent already since earlier times. However, the war of the 1980s did appear different because some reports indicated a massive deployment of air power and mechanized military formations. Related reporting nearly stopped in 1989, when the government of the Union of the Soviet Socialist Republics (USSR, also 'Soviet Union') announced it would cease supporting the Ethiopian government. Less than two years later, dramatic photographs and news surfaced about insurgents entering the Ethiopian capital, about the Ethiopian Air Force (EtAF) flying fierce air strikes in response, and then the downfall of the government. The area subsequently descended below the attention of the international media, and it appeared that the two countries that emerged from the earlier war – Ethiopia, and a newly-independence Eritrea – were close allies. However, in 1998, precisely these two nations fought the last conventional conflict of the 20th Century, but also the first of the 21st Century. This time, rumours began spreading about even bigger battles, deployment of some of the most modern military technology of Russian origin, and air battles between such advanced fighter-bomber types as the Mikoyan i Gurevich MiG-29 and Sukhoi Su-27.

Though all of this time, relatively few hard facts became known about the military history of a decades-long and obviously massive conflict between Ethiopia and Eritrea. Indeed, to many interested foreign observers, it appeared de-facto 'impossible' that two nations widely considered as some of the poorest on the African continent, could have run military conflicts of the reported size and scope. This began to change only over the last decade, when the first authoritative accounts were published – foremost by Ethiopian researchers. Rather suddenly, they provided an image of a constantly growing Ethiopian military of the 1980s and its involvement in a decades-long, massive war against an uprising in Eritrea. This was far from all: through such publications it became obvious that the conflict nowadays colloquially known as the Eritrean Liberation War, fought 1961-1991, included a full spectrum of warfare: from almost 'classic', so-called counter-insurgency (COIN) operations, via mechanized warfare in the desert, to conventional mountain warfare. Furthermore, it became known that campaigns of this war were often conducted by powerful, comparatively well-equipped forces, led by well-educated commanders that followed carefully designed military plans – even if operating on basis of what was largely a home-grown doctrine.

As Ethiopia gradually re-built its military – especially during the so-called Badme War with Eritrea, fought in 1998-2001 – and then got involved in fighting in the ruined Somalia too, it became obvious that this country was a military powerhouse of the African continent. This made it even more important to study not only the performance of its military in the course of earlier wars, but the influence of earlier military traditions and military history in general upon modern-day military thinking in the country too.

The following volume is the result of years of – often troublesome – research about related issues. The narrative it offers is based on information from diverse sources: works by Ethiopian scholars like Fantahun Ayele and Gebru Tareke were crucial. However, other sources – including some of the Ethiopian participants in these wars – became available over the time, while also a plethora of documents related to the Badme War was subsequently released by the United Nations (UN). Even with all of the materials in question, some details – especially those related to the Badme War – stubbornly remain unknown: the archive of the Ethiopian Air Force remains outside the public reach. Due to multiple ongoing tensions on the national and international plain alike, this is unlikely to change in the foreseeable future.

Short History of Eritrea

Situated at the north-eastern corner of Africa, close to the Arabian Peninsula and on the coast of the Indian Ocean, the Gulf of Aden, and the Red Sea, and containing ports and airfields that connect routes of intercontinental significance, the Horn of Africa is of substantial strategic importance. Stretching from Sudan in the north and west, southwards to Kenya, and to Djibouti in the east, Ethiopia is the biggest country in this area. With its geography and population described extensively in Volume 1 of this series, it is sufficient to say that as a country of isolated mountain plateaus and desert lowlands, Ethiopia's population of about 25-30 million in the 1960s-1980s was culturally diverse and spoke about 70 different languages, mostly of the Semitic and Cushitic branches of the Afro-Asiatic family.

Having a history closely intermingled with that of Ethiopia is Eritrea – a country that took its name from the Latin for Red Sea – Mare Erythraeum. Geographically, the area within its modern-day borders consists of the humid Red Sea littoral, a cooler, better-watered central highland area (where its capitol Asmara is located), and the hot, dry lowlands next to the Sudanese border. The population was always unevenly distributed, with most living in the highlands, or in the relatively hospitable territory around the port of Massawa – and was always deeply divided based on language, ethnic affiliations, and way of life.

Apparently on the fringe of what used to be the centuries-old Ethiopian Empire, Eritrea has a tumultuous history of invasions and internal strife dating back to the 2nd Century BC, when Semitic immigrants founded a kingdom centred on Aksum, in present-day Tigray, with Adulis (nowadays Zula) serving as their main port. Over the time, the Aksumite Kingdom encompassed northern Tigray, the southern Eritrean Highlands, and part of the coast of the Red Sea, thus forming the fundamentals of modern-day Ethiopia. In the 4th Century, the Aksumite Kingdom converted to Christianity, and then continued to prosper until the Islamic expansion in the 7th Century. In the 8th Century, the Aksumites were superseded by the Bejas, who established five kingdoms that dominated most of the modern-day Eritrea, Tigray, and north-eastern Sudan for more than 700 years. In 1528, a Muslim army from the nearby Sultanate of Adal invaded Ethiopia. As well as spreading Islam, the Sultan's fighters defeated whatever forces the Ethiopians put in their way. On the verge of losing his ancient nation, the Negus ('King') Lebna Dengle Dawit II requested help from Portugal, thus making the first contact with the outside world in centuries. The Portuguese expedition led by Cristóvão da Gama arrived in 1541, and helped save Ethiopia, but was then obliged to leave immediately after the defeat of the Muslim army. Despite their defeat, the Ottomans established themselves in control of most of the coastal area by 1557.

The next 300 years of history of this part of Africa were marked by bitter religious conflicts between different Ethiopian rulers and the Jesuits. It was only in 1855 – when Lij Kassa proclaimed himself 'Negus Negusti' ('King of Kings') under the name Tewodros II – that the modernisation and opening of Ethiopia began. Although a ruthless ruler, Tewodros II managed to re-unite Ethiopia while protecting it from the Europeans who were scrambling to secure colonies in Africa, and from the Egyptian Khedivites, who replaced the Ottomans in 1865. Their short-lived occupation was precipitated by an unsuccessful foray into Ethiopia as well as expansion into the Sudan. Tewodros not only resisted the Khedivites fiercely, ultimately forcing them to withdraw, but established Addis Ababa as a new capital, and then fought a short war with the British Empire, in 1867, which ended with Ethiopian defeat during the battle of Magdala (better known as Amba Mariam) – prompting him into suicide.

Following another power struggle, Kassa was crowned as the Emperor Yohannes IV. He rose to power at the time the Red Sea became strategically important due to the opening of the Suez Canal. As Western colonial nations opened political battles for the control over the shores, the British occupied Yemen, and the French took Obock, Asars and Issa (future Djibouti). In 1870, the Italians appeared on the scene and, realising that the Ethiopian control of the area was tentative, managed to buy the port of Asseb from the local Sultan. In 1888, they exploited Yohannes IV's preoccupation with defending Ethiopia from an invasion of dervishes from Sudan and deployed 20,000 troops in the country. Not interested in fighting the newcomers, the Emperor solved all of the disputes – more or less – through negotiations, and granted permission for some 5,000 Italian troops to remain stationed in a part of the Ethiopian Tigray Province along the Red Sea, which over time became known as 'Eritrea' – officially declared an Italian colony in 1892. The next Ethiopian Emperor, Menelik II, signed a treaty with Rome, granting Eritrea to Italy in exchange for 30,000 rifles, ammunition, and several cannons. The Italians declared this treaty as granting them a protectorate over all of Ethiopia, causing another war: this culminated in their humiliating defeat during the battle of Adwa, on 1 March 1896, and a treaty through which Rome recognized the independence of Ethiopia.

Drive for Independence

Looking for a way to re-acquire access to the sea, Emperor Menelik II then made a treaty with France, in 1897, arranging – amongst other things – for a railway to be built connecting the port of Djibouti to Addis Ababa. The first trains ran along this route in 1917. Meanwhile, despite the failure of their designs for Ethiopia, the Italians invested handsomely into Eritrea, constructed roads and railways, introduced modern agriculture, industry, education, and administration. Certainly enough, their efforts were anything other than easy: cultivated land was scarce (only about three percent of the total Eritrean surface area), other natural resources and the domestic market in general were minimal. Grain had to be imported from the Ethiopian hinterland even in the years of good harvest, and Eritrea's greatest agricultural wealth was its livestock. Therefore, Italian colonial authorities in Eritrea initially maintained friendly relations with Ethiopia. Seeking for ways to intensify the local trade and attract some of the Ethiopian goods exported via Djibouti, in 1928, the Italians made a treaty with Ethiopian Emperor Haile Selassie, granting a free trade zone for Ethiopian goods in the port of Asseb. Correspondingly, a road was constructed connecting Asseb with Dese in Ethiopia.

Although the population of Eritrea – meanwhile about equally split into Christians and Muslims – remained deeply divided, the Italians gradually developed their colony to a point where it became possible to establish an army staffed by the locals. By 1934, this included two divisions of regular troops and a number of semi-regular units – primarily consisting of Eritrean Muslims, but of the Somalis, too. Grouped into the Eritrean Army Corps, the 1st and 2nd Eritrean Divisions, and auxiliary units were involved in the Italian invasion of Ethiopia, launched in October 1935. Despite valiant resistance by the Ethiopian military, which was woefully short on modern armament, the Italians – skilfully supported by their Eritrean troops – captured Addis Ababa in May 1936, forcing Emperor Selassie into exile. The war was continued by several Ethiopian armies that remained in the field. Furthermore, only months after Italy's entry into World War II, the British launched multiple attacks into Ethiopia from Kenya and British Somaliland. After successfully outflanking and bluffing far larger Italian units, the British helped a small force of Sudanese and Ethiopian troops to liberate Addis Ababa in May 1941, and enabled Emperor Selassie to make a triumphal return.

The expulsion of the Italians from Ethiopia and Eritrea brought no respite. In 1942, an insurgency erupted in Tigray, in reaction to which Selassie was forced to deploy 35,000 troops to stabilise the situation. Supported by the Royal Air Force (RAF), they put down this revolt in blood in late 1943. Before long, trouble was brewing in Eritrea, too. Because of its status as a former Italian colony, this region came under a UN mandate and British administration, but the Soviet Union stunned Western Allies by requesting a trusteeship over the area at the Potsdam Conference in 1945. The British administrators had encouraged the development of labour units and political parties, and established an elected legislature. Combined with the development introduced by the Italians at earlier times, this resulted in the

Eritreans becoming not only politically conscious, or developing their own political traditions, but also convinced that they had outstripped the rest of Ethiopia in their development. Therefore, when – following the British withdrawal of September 1952 – Emperor Selassie began whittling down the autonomous status of Eritrea, strikes and public demonstrations became common, and the first pro-independence group – the Eritrean Liberation Movement (ELM) – was founded in Sudan in 1958. Selassie reacted by deploying the Ethiopian Army and federating Eritrea to become one of nine provinces of the Ethiopian Union. All independent institutions and political parties were subverted and freedom of speech, press, and assembly suppressed. Even the local dialects were discouraged in favour of Amharic, the official language in Ethiopia. All Eritrean protests were to no avail: although this only provided a boost to the emergence of additional, and then armed separatist movements. In 1962, Eritrea was officially annexed to Ethiopia.

The First Decade of the War

While the viability of Eritrea as an independent state was always under a huge question mark – because the area remained unable to support itself, and heavily dependent on Ethiopian investment – and despite the Ethiopians constructing their biggest refinery at Assab, and one of their biggest cement plants at Massawa, the separatist movements continued to grow in the early 1960s. Initially at least, the separatists were foremost supported by the Muslim herdsmen of the lowlands. The Christians, most of whom were settled agriculturalists in the highlands, were traditionally more amenable to some kind of continuing relationship with Ethiopia. However, the reversion of the Ethiopian government to the hard line on Eritrea greatly increased the support for independence. On the contrary, south-eastern Eritrea, populated by Dankali tribesmen, was largely left to its own devices: Dankalis were renowned for their hostility to any kind of external authority, and thus not only Ethiopians, but Eritrean separatists too had all avoided interfering with them.

The group that was to become most influential in Eritrea of the 1960s came into being as the Eritrean Liberation Front (ELF). Formed in Cairo by Muslim lowlanders, in July 1960, and just like the ELM, the ELF went through a rather moderate phase in its early existence. Indeed, the number of their attacks only gradually grew in intensity, from 4 in 1962, to 27 in 1966. The situation experienced a dramatic change once the ELF's military wing, the Eritrean Liberation Army (ELA), was reorganised along the pattern previously used by the National Liberation Front in Algeria, and then intensified its operations, in early 1967. This prompted the Imperial Ethiopian Army to deploy two brigades into a three-phased counterinsurgency (COIN) operation codenamed Wegaw ('Trash'). While resulting in the arrest of almost anybody suspected for collaboration with or support of insurgents, and large-scale devastation of property, the results of Wegaw remained limited. Generally, the governmental bodies only managed to retain effective control over the towns and major land communications routes, but failed to prevent the expansion of the insurgency.

Although the ELF/ELA successfully neutralised its primary competitor, the ELM, in the mid-1960s, it nearly fell apart

in the early 1970s. However, three splinter groups re-aligned and partially merged to create the Eritrean People's Liberation Front (EPLF), and its armed wing, the Eritrean People's Liberation Army (EPLA) in 1977. Meanwhile, Emperor Selassie was deposed, and a years-long power struggle developed in Addis Ababa. This resulted in a military junta – officially the Provisional Military Administrative Committee (PMAC), colloquially known as the Derg (or Dergue) – presided over by Colonel Mengistu Haile Mariam (former officer of the elite 3rd Infantry Division) establishing itself in power, but also in a widespread disorganisation and disengagement of the Ethiopian military in Eritrea. Emboldened, the insurgents launched a series of offensives in the course of which the EPLF and the ELF established themselves in control of most of Eritrea other than Asmara, Massawa, Asseb, Barentu and Senafe.

EPLA insurgents entering the 'airport' of Asmara, in 1991, where they captured the empty hulk of the An-12B with serial number 1506, visible in the background. (Mark Lepko Collection)

Ethiopian Counteroffensives

Meanwhile, another insurgency erupted in Tigray, where the Tigray People's Liberation Front (TPLF) was established in February 1975, in protest against the state of backwardness in which this area has fallen. The TPLF's first armed action took place in August 1975, and the organisation subsequently continued to grow thanks not only to support from local peasantry, but also from abroad. However, for the first decade of its existence, the Tigreyan insurgency was foremost preoccupied with fighting diverse of its rivals instead of the central government.

Until early 1978, the bulk of the Ethiopian military was committed against Somalia, which invaded the Ogaden region in summer of the previous year. The EPLF and the ELF thus continued advancing until nearly 80% of Eritrea was under their control. However, understanding that the loss of Eritrea would be a bitter blow for the country and isolate it from approach to the sea, as soon as it secured a victory against Somalia, the Derg began turning its attention upon Eritrea. In early 1978, it established the 90,000-strong Second Revolutionary Army (SRA), and then launched a multi-pronged offensive with the aim of crushing the ELF and the EPLF. Initiated in June 1978, this operation lasted for nearly three months, and resulted in the Ethiopians clearing most of southern and central Eritrea of insurgents. After resting and re-organizing their forces, they attacked again in November 1978, this time aiming to recover Akordat, Afabet, and Keren. Next, the Ethiopian military secured the road connecting Asmara and Massawa. However, and although managing to take Alghena further north, they failed to capture Nakfa; the very epicentre of the Eritrean insurgency and the EPLF/EPLA in particular. Instead, and despite further Ethiopian offensives of 1979 and 1980, the EPLF was able to fortify the sizeable area around this town, the so-called Sahel Redoubt, and then finish the – meanwhile much weakened – ELF/ELA, forcing its survivors to flee to Sudan.

Following another COIN campaign in Ogaden, run by the First Revolutionary Army (FRA) in mid-1980, the Ethiopians returned in force to Eritrea in 1981, this time aiming to finish off the EPLF/EPLA with a particularly massive onslaught: Operation Red Star. Proceeded by a full month of unprecedented air strikes, Red Star was launched in February 1982, and initially resulted in significant advances. Ultimately, the Ethiopian assault once again became bogged down in the elaborate complex of fortifications protecting the Sahel Redoubt, consisting of miles-long trenches combined with expertly concealed bunkers.

With hindsight, the failure of the Red Star campaign – concluded in June 1982, following a staggering loss of 37,136 Ethiopian casualties – proved a turning point in the war in Eritrea. The operation bled and broke the Ethiopian army, and converted this conflict from one the Derg hoped to end quickly, into a never-ending battle of attrition which Ethiopia was actually unable to support. Almost unsurprisingly, mutinies erupted in multiple units of the army, the leadership of which became divided due to mutual distrust. Ignoring the worsening of its general position, the Derg quickly reorganised the military and launched another attack on the Sahel Redoubt – the Stealth Offensive – in early 1983. Indeed, this operation took the insurgents by surprise and initially achieved significant advances. However, once again, the

Ethiopians suffered massive casualties while assaulting heavily fortified positions of the EPLA, hopelessly exhausting themselves by June 1983.

At least as alarming should have been the fact that the Derg's 'hearts and minds' policy – including significant investment into infrastructure-rehabilitation projects, and a resettlement of rural population – failed, too. On the contrary, violent repression by the Ethiopian security apparatus ruined the government's standing in the population, while making its opponents ever more popular. Not only that the EPLF survived in its Sahel Redoubt, but by 1984 the TPLF controlled most of the countryside in the Tigray, while Adigrat and Shire were de-facto under siege. Ironically, it was exactly around this time that the EPLF ceased providing support for the TPLF and blocked its only road connection with Sudan in 1985. However, with the Ethiopian military remaining concentrated in Eritrea, the Tigreyan insurgency had little to fear: indeed, the threat to its survival was soon to significantly decrease.[2]

EPLF on the Advance

Although taking more than a year to recover its strength following the Red Star campaign and the Stealth Offensive, subsequently, the EPLF found itself in possession of the strategic initiative. In January 1984, it captured Tesseney and Ali Ghidir, thus securing the land connection between the Sahel Redoubt and Sudan. Only a week later, the insurgents took the Ethiopian military by surprise through securing the Alghena area, on the coast of the Red Sea. Next, they attempted to lessen the pressure exercised upon them by the EtAF thorough raiding air bases of Asmara and Massawa.

Top Ethiopian generals and commanders of Operation Red Star (from left to right): Brigadier-General Techane Mesfin (EtAF), Major-General Eshetu Gebremariam, Major General Wubetu Tsegaye, Major-General Woldeye Gebrehana, Colonel Bacha Hunde (EtAF), Lieutenant-Colonel Amsalu Gebrezgi, and Lieutenant-Commander Afework Takele. (EtaF via S. N.)

Although receiving timely warnings from its intelligence services, the Ethiopian military failed to react: eight MiGs and two helicopters were destroyed at Asmara on 20 May 1984, while one MiG was destroyed and two damaged at Massawa, on 14 January 1986. Furthermore, in July 1985, the EPLA assaulted and captured Barentu.

The Derg reacted by re-deploying significant reinforcements to this area, and recovered the town by the end of the month in Operation Red Sea. Emboldened by this success, the Ethiopians then launched a new offensive on the Sahel Redoubt, Operation Bahra Nagash. Although marred by logistical problems, this enterprise yielded the capture of Algena early on, before their advance was stalled by bitter resistance. After two weeks of stalemate, the Ethiopians changed their main axis of advance and their Nadew Command launched a night assault from another direction. However, having the advantage of an inner line of communications, the EPLA reacted by quickly re-deploying its units to the southern frontline. Operation Bahra Nagash thus ended in similar fashion to all the earlier enterprises of this kind: with massive Ethiopian casualties.

Immediately afterwards, the EPLA exploited growing chaos, disorganisation, and near-mutiny of the Nadew Command to launch an advance in a southern direction. By May 1986, the road connection between Asmara and Massawa was interrupted again, and both air bases put under insurgent artillery fire. Follow-up actions through 1987 were small by their dimensions, but effective in weakening and creating further rifts within the Ethiopian military. Unsurprisingly, the Nadew Command collapsed under EPLA's attacks in December of the same year, and no amount of purges of officers or appointments of new commanders could help recover the situation any more. In March 1988, the EPLA infiltrated the positions of multiple Ethiopian units protecting the road between Afabet and Keren, and thus isolated the remnants of the Nadew Command. When these attempted to withdraw along the road in a southern direction, they ran into a trap between the Mashalit and Ad Sharum Passes. Following a loss of nearly 3,000 killed, over 6,000 wounded, and 3,000 missing in action; having hundreds of its armoured vehicles captured or destroyed; and losing extensive stocks of supplies in what became known as the Battle of Afabet, the Nadew Command was virtually destroyed. This victory not only opened the way for further advances of the EPLF in the direction

of Keren, but foremost proved a major propaganda coup for the Eritreans. Indeed, trying to close the giant gap in its frontlines, the Ethiopian military was forced to withdraw its garrisons from Barentu and Agordat. Although the insurgents suffered extensive casualties during this campaign, and while Mengistu subsequently ordered the SRA into a new offensive, and this even managed to recover the Mashalit Pass, in May 1988, the Eritrean victory at Afabet marked the beginning of the end of the Ethiopian hold on Eritrea, and of the Derg government in Addis Ababa.

ELA insurgents with a captured M41 Walker Buldog light tank of the Ethiopian Army in 1978. The EPLA also captured at least one US-made M113 armoured personnel carrier and pressed it into service, during the same year. (Mark Lepko Collection)

EPLA combatants with a PKM machine gun, in a dominating position, in 1988. (EPLF)

CHAPTER 2
BATTLE FOR TIGRAY

During the first half of 1988, both the EPLF and the TPLF had realised that – despite their ideological differences – they had much to gain from resuming cooperation. The potential advantages became obvious in March 1988, when the TPLF exploited the void created by the re-deployment of the elite 3rd Infantry Division to Eritrea and captured several towns in Tigray. In the course of the fighting between 28 and 31 March, the Tigrayan insurgents inflicted severe casualties upon the 16th and 17th Infantry Divisions, destroyed nine T-55 main

battle tanks (MBTs), nine ZU-23 anti-aircraft cannons, and numerous other heavy and light weapons. By April, the TPLF found itself in control of the entirety of Tigray, except for its capital – Mekelle – and a handful of other towns. Next, the Tigrayans spread their activity into the Gondar and Wello provinces. Correspondingly, the representatives of the two insurgent movements met for four days in Khartoum, and agreed to issue a joint communiqué, announcing that henceforth they would fight the Derg together.[3]

However, the insurgents were not the only ones to exploit the tools of diplomacy in those days. After the disaster of Afabet, Mengistu accelerated ongoing negotiations with Somalia: Ethiopia had been in a state of war with its eastern neighbour since the Ogaden War of 1977-1978, and each side was supporting insurgent groups active in the others' country. Already facing growing opposition at home, the Somali strongman, Major-General Sia'ad Barre, was keen to improve relations with Ethiopia. Therefore, on 16 May 1988, an agreement was signed between Addis Ababa and Mogadishu to officially end this conflict, exchange prisoners of war, and de-militarise a strip 15 kilometres to either side of the border. In this fashion, the Derg was able to free significant portions of its military and re-deploy them to other parts of the country.[4]

In similar fashion, the Derg also took care to lessen tensions with the government in Khartoum – although that effort proved less successful: neither Ethiopia nor Sudan had ever completely stopped supporting insurgents threatening the other side. In particular, Addis Ababa always supported the Southern People's Liberation Army (SPLA), established in 1983 and led by Colonel John Garang, because this proved a useful tool to punish Khartoum for its support for the EPLF, TPLF, and other armed groups in Ethiopia. Exploiting the weak Sudanese air defences, the EtAF even deployed its helicopters to haul supplies to SPLA bases in southern Sudan, enabling it to launch two significant offensives: one in the Blue Nile Province, in November 1987, and another in Eastern Equatoria Province, in early 1988. This support was slightly decreased following the 'warming' of relations between Addis Ababa and Khartoum, in mid-1988. However, by then the EPLF and the TPLF proved far more self-sufficient than the SPLA. Furthermore, this détente ended when Brigadier-General Omar Hassan al-Bashir established himself in power during the coup of June 1989.

Foremost, all of these diplomatic efforts proved of limited use due to a detrimental affair of July 1988, when – during his visit to Moscow – Mengistu Haile Mariam was informed by Mikhail Gorbachev, the General Secretary of the Communist Party of the Soviet Union and the head of state, that Moscow would greatly reduce the flow of arms and ammunition sold to Ethiopia. Indeed, Gorbachev went as far as to suggest to the Derg to find a negotiated settlement with the diverse insurgent movements. Although turning down such ideas, writing was now on the wall for Mengistu's rule over Ethiopia.[5]

Reorganisation of the Ethiopian Army

In the light of new relations with its neighbours, in April 1988 the Derg reorganised the Ethiopian Army. Normalisation of relations with Somalia had enabled the transfer of units from the FRA in Ogaden, to the SRA and the Third Revolutionary Army (TRA), responsible for the provinces of Assab, Tigray, Wello, Gondar and Gojjam. Much of the transfer of troops to the SRA was undertaken with help of EtAF transports, and chartered airliners, in an intensive aerial bridge, run from 19 March until 26 September 1988. This included 234 flights by An-12 transports and 380 by passenger aircraft of Ethiopian Airlines. Subsequently, the very small Fourth Revolutionary Army (FORA) became responsible for protecting the borders not only with Kenya, but also with Somalia and Sudan. In place of the former commands, thirteen corps commands were established, each of which was assigned to one of the army-headquarters. Moreover, intensive efforts were made to enlist additional troops, and to recall former national servicemen, in order to reinforce depleted formations (the resulting structure is detailed in Table 1). The total manpower thus reached 388,926 officers and other ranks, making the Ethiopian military the largest in sub-Saharan Africa, and certainly more than two times the size of the combined forces of Somalia and Sudan.[6]

Considering the terrible drought that caused the death of hundreds of thousands of peasants in the north of the country to famine-related causes in 1984 and 1985, such an increase in manpower of the Ethiopian military might appear surprising. However, the Derg effectively used the famine to strengthen its position through channelling most of the massive outpouring of aid from the international community into government-controlled areas – while vehemently opposing all efforts to provide aid to the drought-victims in regions controlled by the insurgents. Furthermore, the government re-settled nearly one million people from the contested northern regions to western and central Ethiopia, explaining this decision as a consequence of the devastation of their homeland and the necessity to re-settle people to more fertile lowland areas. Finally, the Derg used military force to disrupt the flow of food from Sudan to the insurgent-controlled areas and to stem the tide of refugees into Sudanese relief camps – because both these flows had been exploited by the insurgents to sustain themselves. With the military always getting first crack at goods purchased commercially – but agricultural commodities supplied by farmers and state-owned farms to meet government quotas, too – many Ethiopians found it an interesting incentive to join the military.[7]

Moreover, this growth of the Ethiopian military was made possible by the temporary improvement of relations between Addis Ababa and Moscow in the mid-1980s. Part of this was the result of Moscow – in attempt to institutionalise Soviet influence, and in hope that a government dominated by civilians would be easier to influence than a military junta – pressed the Derg into creating a Communist Party. Certainly enough, Mengistu packed that party's leadership with members of his military clique.

A mortar team of the TPLF undergoing training. (Bahir Dar War Memorial)

However, the Soviet concerns that such activities might arouse the suspicions of the Ethiopian leader (renowned for his constant dissatisfaction with the level and quality of Soviet military and economic aid) – prompted them to tolerate his behaviour and avoid attempting to actively strengthen their favourites. On the contrary, high-level Soviet military officials continued paying regular visits to Ethiopia, and arms shipments continued to arrive all through the period 1984-1988 (including the times of the famine crisis), thus underlining Moscow's commitment as the Derg's primary backer. Unsurprisingly, one contemporary US intelligence assessments observed:

> 'Mengistu's strategy for dealing with those most directly affected by the famine – the rural population – appears to us aimed more at using the crisis to weaken the insurgencies than at meeting the food needs of starving peasants. The regime has established feeding centres at major cities and towns under its control in the north, but has refused to authorise the movement of relief supplies to insurgent-held areas and has hindered international efforts to reach those most at risk...'[8]

However, the Soviets had meanwhile recognized the fact that any kind of a foreign meddling or intervention was likely to result in a surge of patriotism that united even the constantly-quarrelling Ethiopians. Indeed, they often found themselves confronted with strong opposition to their influence in Ethiopian domestic and military affairs: eventually, Moscow was forced into the realisation that most Ethiopian officers were openly dissatisfied not only with the level of economic and military assistance, but repayment terms for arms purchased by Addis Ababa, too, and that the majority of them considered the Soviet assistance as a mere stopgap measure designed to ensure continued Ethiopian dependence on Soviet aid. Correspondingly, Soviet advisors were ordered to maintain a low profile. Nevertheless, the Soviet Military Advisory Group in Ethiopia meanwhile had its top advisers assigned to the headquarters of each of the Revolutionary Armies, between 10 and 15 assigned to each corps and divisional headquarters, and additional officers serving as advisors to commanders of Ethiopian brigades.[9]

While the SRA benefited greatly from this reorganisation, growing to a total of 163,192 officers and other ranks, it was still badly short on equipment. For example, in all of 1988, it received only 95 Gaz-66 and Ural-375 trucks out of 650 it originally requested.[10]

Table 1: Ethiopian Army Order of Battle, April-July 1988

Army	Corps	Manpower
First Revolutionary Army	601st and 602nd	36,635
Second Revolutionary Army	606th, 607th, 608th, 609th, 610th	163,192
Third Revolutionary Army	603rd, 604th, 605th	104,938
Fourth Revolutionary Army	611th, 612th, 614th	23,040

At the Zenith

Although deliveries of additional aircraft and helicopters from the USSR remained unpredictable, the Ethiopian Air Force reached its peak strength ever by 1988. It included about 7,000 officers and other ranks, more than 110 combat aircraft, about 20 transport aircraft, and the Army Aviation Battalion was now equipped with about 60 Mil Mi-8, Mi-17, Mi-24 and Mi-35 helicopters, the crews of which were trained to provide close air support. These were organised into 24 squadrons, distributed between five 'commands', as described in Table 2. In addition to controlling multiple operational units, each of the commands had its own training squadron, and its own search and rescue flight equipped with at least one Mi-8 helicopter. The backbone of the fighter-bomber fleet remained about 70 MiG-21bis' and about 40 MiG-23BNs, the last batches of which were delivered by ship via the ports of Asseb and Massawa in 1983 – instead of on board Soviet transport aircraft, as in earlier times, in order to keep their acquisition cost low.[11] One of the commands was actually seconded to the Navy, which operated a small air arm equipped with two Mil Mi-14 helicopters, though no Mi-24s or Mi-35s.[12]

Although gaining in strength and experience, Ethiopian units equipped with Mi-8s, Mi-24s, Mi-35s, MiG-21s and MiG-23s continued experiencing similar personnel and logistic-related problems that affected their operational effectiveness – especially

An-12 transports of the EtAF played a crucial role in re-deploying large contingents of the Ethiopian Army from Ogaden to the north of the country: between March and September 1988 they flew 234 related sorties. (Herve Dessallier via Albert Grandolini)

in sustained operations – as described in detail in Volume 1. While a large number of pilots and ground personnel returned from their training in the USSR in the early 1980s, many were still not available for combat operations, because – due to the shortcomings of Soviet flight training, foremost limited flying time and poor instruction in aerial manoeuvring – they first all had to be completely re-trained. Moreover, continuous delays in provision of spare parts, defective components, an inefficient logistic system, and the refusal of Soviet advisors to train the Ethiopian technical personnel in undertaking on-the-spot repairs, resulted in less than 50% of aircraft and helicopters being operational on average.[13]

The transport fleet – bolstered through the acquisition of several Antonov An-26s – was in constant and intensive service, as was the helicopter fleet, reinforced through the acquisition of an unknown number of Mil Mi-17 assault and transport helicopters.[14]

Table 2: Ethiopian Air Force Order of Battle, 1988-1991

Unit	Base	Notes
1st Command	Debre Zeit AB	major operational base, housing up to 8 squadrons equipped of MiG-21s and all transport units; maintaining detachments at Azazo and Gambela
2nd Command	Asmara IAP	up to 4 squadrons of MiG-21s, MiG-23s, and diverse helicopters; maintaining detachments at Agordat, Keren, Mekelle and Asseb
3rd Command	Dire Dawa AB	major training base, controlling the Basic Training School (SF.260s) and Advanced Training School (L-39s), and one or two MiG-21 and MiG-23 squadrons; maintaining detachments at Gode
4th Command	Bahir Dar AB	major MiG-23BN base; maintaining detachments at Asmara and Asseb
6th Command	Lidetta AB	Army Aviation Battalion including 4 or 5 squadrons flying Mi-8/17s, Mi-24s, Mi-35s, and DHC-6s
	Asseb IAP	logistic hub and home base for two Mi-14 helicopters assigned to the Navy

Soviet Military Bases in Ethiopia

During the mid-1980s, the Cold War reached its new peak, and thus – and because of the country's strategic position and importance – any Ethiopia-related discussions between military observers in the West were regularly touching the topic of Soviet military presence in that country. With hindsight, the conclusion is that the Soviet military presence in Ethiopia was actually minimal. Indeed, contrary to what might be expected, the Soviets were rather slow to develop bases in Ethiopia. In 1978, they began developing a modest facility on one of Ethiopia's isolated islands in the Dahlak archipelago of the Red Sea. They positioned a 7,700-tonnes floating dry-dock (previously stationed in Somalia), added housing for some 200 personnel, two floating piers, petroleum storage facilities, helicopter pads, and other necessities to their base, which subsequently averaged 80-100 ship visits a year (primarily by warships of the Indian Ocean Squadron of the Soviet Navy). However, they never received the same degree of access to the ports of Assab and Massawa, which had larger and better facilities than Dahlak.

Since 1980, the Soviets periodically deployed two Ilyushin Il-38 (ASCC code 'May') maritime patrol and anti-submarine warfare aircraft at Yohannes IV airport outside Asmara. These were supported by a pair of An-12 transports, and primarily used for reconnaissance missions against Western warships in the northwest Indian Ocean.

Therefore, the Soviet military presence in Ethiopia remained very limited. A mere 1,700 advisors were in the country for most of the 1980s. Their primary tasks included advising senior Ethiopian officers in planning and conducting major combat operations and administrative undertakings, provision of technical and logistic support of complex weapons systems and training of weapons-system specialists, and combat training for brigade and division-sized units.[15]

Soviet Mi-8 helicopter taking-off from Asmara airport in the mid-1980s. Visible in the rear are two hardened aircraft shelters, each with one of EtAF MiG-21s inside. (Pit Weinert Collection)

Although busy fighting a war, the EtAF still found time to take part in occasional parades in Addis Ababa. This photograph shows a formation of MiG-23BNs led by Mesfin Haile (MA), and including aircraft flown by Tadesse Muluneh (SL), Teshale Zewdie (TD), and Nebiyu Abraha (NB). (EtAF via S. N.)

While not present in Ethiopia in large units, Soviet instructors were attached to every squadron of the EtAF, and the headquarters of every brigade, division, and corps of the Ethiopian Army. This photograph shows one of the Ethiopian MiG-21UM conversion-trainers (serial number 2003) and its crews, together with their Soviet advisors. (Pit Weinert Collection)

Counter-value Doctrine

Although Ethiopian MiG-21 and MiG-23 pilots had repeatedly demonstrated high levels of competence when providing CAS to the ground forces during the mid-1980s, most of the Soviet advisors assigned to the EtAF as of 1988 had still served with units operating fighter-bombers. While the exact extent of their influence upon the general conduct of combat operations remains unclear, there is little doubt that after the defeat at Afabet, the Ethiopian Air Force began applying tactics that closely resembled that of the Soviet air force in Afghanistan, or the one applied by Soviet advisors in Mozambique of the early 1980s: contrary to the traditional counter-force doctrine – one of fighting the enemy military – the EtAF began applying the so-called counter-value doctrine: one of attacking the civilian population in insurgent-controlled areas.

The primary targets for an increasing number of its air strikes became markets: places crucial for the economic life of the population in rural areas, especially at the time of food shortage still experienced in much of northern Ethiopia. While relatively economic in terms of bombs and fuel spent, and the ease with which such 'targets' were found – then, contrary to the insurgents, which were mobile and operating from well-concealed positions, and thus hard to hit – air strikes on markets had proved to have particularly damaging effects: not only that they caused a marked depression in trade, drove many small merchants out of business, but they also deprived farmers of consumer goods. Another aim of this campaign was to instil fear into the civilian population: persistent bombing not only imposed enormous practical problems, but also demoralised civilians, forcing thousands of them to flee, in turn denying the insurgents the ability to control the local population. This was of particular importance for the Derg, which – like many governments in similar position – defined itself through the level of control it exercised over the Ethiopian population.

While air strikes on the civilian population in Eritrea did occur at earlier times (at least since 1985), and had already caused the death of hundreds, if not thousands, and although certainly intentional, there is no clear evidence that they were a part of an orchestrated campaign. On the contrary, starting in early 1988, such attacks were flown regularly and intensively. Early that year, the Derg not only declared a State of Emergency in Eritrea and Tigray, but also declared a strip 10 kilometres wide along the coast and the Sudanese border as a 'prohibited area', and ordered the EtAF into an intensive campaign of bombardments. Contrary to earlier times, when MiG-21s and MiG-23BNs used to deploy high-explosive/fragmentation bombs, during this campaign they began deploying Soviet-made RBK-250 and RBK-500 cluster bomber units (CBUs) filled with incendiaries.

Examples of intentional air strikes on civilians soon grew into the dozens and then the hundreds. When air strikes on markets did not show immediate effects, the EtAF widened its campaign to include activities of such humanitarian organisations associated with insurgents as the Eritrean Relief Association (ERA) and the Relief Society of Tigray (REST). With assistance from international relief agencies, these organisations were providing food and other assistance to the civilian population in areas controlled by the insurgents. Correspondingly, Ethiopian fighter-bombers began regular attacks on relief convoys moving in from Sudan. Initially, Addis Ababa explained such actions with claims that the ERA and the REST were bringing military supplies to the insurgents. However, the EtAF soon began striking well-known centres for relief distribution, even those run by such organisations as the Red Cross of Ethiopia. Ultimately, its campaign against civilians in Eritrea and Tigray reached such proportions, and caused so much damage and suffering, that it exposed many of the pilots involved to prosecution after the fall of the Derg in 1991, and is one of the primary reasons for the majority of EtAF veterans refusing to discuss their experiences from this war to this day.

The first to get moving after the Ethiopian defeat at Afabet was the TPLF. In March 1988, it captured Wukro, in eastern Tigray. This town acted as the centre for relief distribution by the International Committee of the Red Cross (ICRC): although the latter subsequently re-launched the distribution of food according to the schedule already agreed with the government, on 8 April 1988, Ethiopian fighter-bombers bombed the town and the ICRC site, killing over 100 civilians that had gathered there. One of the related reports cited:

> 'The ICRC distribution site, with a huge, clearly marked red cross tent, is just on the edge of the town. The ICRC representative of Adigrat, who had taken over responsibility for Wukro after it was controlled by the TPLF, arrived in the late morning…with his mobile radio he sent an open message to the ICRC headquarters in Addis Ababa, giving details on the upcoming distribution… At 1400hrs, MiGs appeared and started bombing, very close to the orphan-center. The building caught fire immediately, and the roof collapsed… in this building, 52 dead bodies were counted…While people from the distribution site and orphan center were fleeing, the MiGs returned and bombed with cluster shells [sic]. In only one street, I counted five big bomb craters.'[16]

Addis Ababa subsequently declared that all those killed were insurgents. In similar fashion, the EtAF hit Afabet, Agordat, and Anseba in Eritrea, during the same month.[17] In April 1988, the TPLF overran the town of Axum, in northern Tigray, where it captured an abandoned Douglas DC-3 of the Ethiopian Airlines (registration ET-AGT). Because it had only one operational engine and was thus unflyable, the insurgents never made use of this aircraft: it was destroyed in an attack by two MiG-23BNs on 2 May.

On 25 May 1988, the TPLF assaulted the town of Korem and overwhelmed the local garrison in the course of a five-hour long battle. Two days later, the TPLF attacked the nearby town of Maychew – headquarters of the 1st Infantry Division of the 605th Corps, and defended by the 117th Infantry Brigade. The defences collapsed even quicker this time. The army thus lost not only the road linking Mekelle with Addis Ababa, or the Commander of the 1st Infantry Division (Colonel Haylu Yohannes), but also three T-55 MBTs and 12 other armoured vehicles, 11 artillery pieces and 4 ZU-23 anti-aircraft cannons. The EtAF reacted by bombing Wukro again, and then Mensura, Halhal, Adigrat, and Afabet in Eritrea.[18]

The fin of a Soviet-made FAB-250M-62 bomb deployed by an EtAF MiG fighter-bomber in an attempt to hit a farmer working his field in an insurgent-controlled area. (Albert Grandolini Collection)

Due to its longer endurance, the MiG-23BN became the primary means of the EtAF's 'counter-value' campaign applied against Eritrea and Tigray in the period 1988-1991. Although of poor quality, this photograph shows one of the last few MiG-23BNs delivered to Ethiopia (serial number 1302), armed with a pair of UB-32-57 pods for unguided rockets. (Pit Weinert Collection)

Operation Adwa

This sudden foray of the TPLF might have been an attempt to pre-empt the Ethiopian large-scale offensive, which was meanwhile clearly in the making, even more so because the Tigrayans understood that while through most of 1978-1988 period the Derg was preoccupied with the destruction of the EPLF, now it might try to deliver the next major blow against them. Indeed, in the aftermath of the defeat at Afabet, the Derg not only reformed the military, but also revised its strategy. Correspondingly, it concluded it had to first destroy the TPLF before it could concentrate all of its attention and forces against the EPLF. This became the aim of Operation Adwa, the ultimate goal of which was to seize the TPLF's main base at Adi Ramets in a mountainous and isolated part of the Gondar Province. The base in question was subjected to repeated air strikes by the EtAF, but proved ever harder to find, because the TPLF went to great extents in order to conceal its headquarters, support and training facilities, and its major depots.[19]

Tasked with Operation Adwa were the 603rd Corps in Gondar Province, and the 604th Corps in Tigray, while the 605th Corps in Wello was to secure their rear areas. Theoretically, these three formations were to be controlled by the TRA, commanded by Major-General Mulatu Negash. However, as so often before and after, Mengistu compromised the chain of command by dispatching his favourite, Captain Lagesse Asfaw to Tigray, accredited with full powers over all the other authorities in Tigray. The reason for this decision was Mengistu's trust in Asfaw, who 'distinguished' himself during the 'Red Terror' campaign in Addis Ababa of 1976-1977. Furthermore, he was not only a widely feared character but also shared Mengistu's propensity to meddle in military operational issues despite lack of qualifications.

With hindsight, it can be concluded that already the arrival of Captain Asfaw in Mekelle, on 3 June 1988, irrevocably flawed the efficiency of TRA's command, even before this embarked on a difficult mission. Another problem facing Operation Adwa was the fact that it was to begin in June, mid-way through the rainy season, and thus at the time that mobility was greatly impeded by rains and muddy ground. Finally, the Derg grossly underestimated the TPLA: although certainly less powerful than the EPLA: the EPLA, it had a force of 20,000 well-trained and highly disciplined regular fighters organised in about a dozen brigades, was not only supported by about a dozen tanks, nine other armoured vehicles and 42 artillery pieces, but could also be quickly reinforced by about the same number of militiamen. Finally, except for the TPLF, at least five other insurgent movements were active in the TRA's area of responsibility as of early 1988, all of which were likely to cooperate if there was a need, despite their mutual disagreements (for a detailed order of battle of the TRA as of this period, see Table 3).[20]

The TRA opened its onslaught on 5 June 1988, with a two-pronged operation to reopen the road connecting Mekelle with Addis Ababa. 9th Infantry Division, which had travelled by sea from Massawa to Asseb and then by road to Dessie, attacked in the direction of Maychew, while the 4th Infantry Division formed the other part of the pincer by advancing from Mekelle. After some very fierce fighting, the two units recaptured Korem and Maychew. On 20 June 1988, the TRA then opened the actual Operation Adwa by another pincer attack of the 604th Corps: one by the 4th and 9th Divisions' advance on Adigrat along the road from Mekelle, and the other by the 16th Infantry Division's advance from Maychew on Abiy Addi. Confronted with this attack, the TPLF opted for its usual tactics of avoiding the decisive battle: instead, it withdrew while fighting multiple rear-guard actions, and occasionally harassing its enemy by flanking counterattacks. Nevertheless, the 16th Infantry had to fight a bitter battle for Samre, from 20 to 22 June, before it was able to take Abyi Addi, three days later. Finally, the 4th and 9th Divisions secured Adigrat on 28 June 1988. Overall, the Ethiopians suffered 1,071 casualties by that point in time.

After securing the rubble that once used to be Abyi Addi and Adigrat, the two main forces of the 604th Corps continued their advance in the direction of Adwa. This town was secured following a pitched battle against the TPLF's rear-guards, entrenched in the surrounding hills, on 29 June. The 604th Corps then pushed further along the road in the northern direction, taking Aksum and, on 3 July 1988, Shire. The three non-motorised divisions thus advanced for nearly 900 kilometres within less than one month.

Table 3: TRA Order of Battle, June 1988

603rd Corps	604th Corps	605th Corps
7th Infantry Division	4th Infantry Division	1st Infantry Division
15th Infantry Brigade	9th Infantry Division	2nd Infantry Brigade
17th Infantry Brigade	16th Infantry Division	16th Infantry Brigade
19th Infantry Brigade	103rd Commando Division	100th Infantry Brigade
33rd Infantry Brigade		117th Infantry Brigade
114th Infantry Brigade		140th Infantry Brigade
115th Infantry Brigade		142nd Infantry Brigade
136th Infantry Brigade		

A column of TPLF insurgents on advance in northern Tigray in 1988. (Bahir Dar War Memorial)

Massacre in Hausien

Despite this success, the EtAF meanwhile subjected multiple towns of Tigray to some of the most savage air raids of this war. On 8 and 10 June 1988, Seqota and Amdo were bombed, and up to a dozen people killed. On 12 June, the EtAF destroyed a REST convoy in the Dejena area. On 14 and 15 June, two air strikes hit Samre, killing 17 and destroying more than a third of the town. Ruba Kaza, Tsegede, Samre again, Shire, Dande, and Raya were raided on 16, 18, 19, and 20 June, causing dozens of deaths and hundreds of casualties. However, probably the worst attack of the conflict hit Hausien on 22 June 1988.

The market in this town attracted people from all parts of Tigray, resulting in the place being packed with several thousands of people, animals, stocks of grain, salt, coffee, and other commodities. Although Hausien was attacked eight times by mid-1988, the residents did not consider themselves at serious risk because the area was not controlled by insurgents: on the contrary, most market-goers came from areas controlled by the government. Therefore – and contrary to the practice of running markets by night meanwhile introduced in several places in Eritrea – the weekly market in Hausien continued to be held during daylight hours.

At about 1000 hrs two EtAF helicopters approached at low altitude and circled the area for about half an hour. They were replaced by

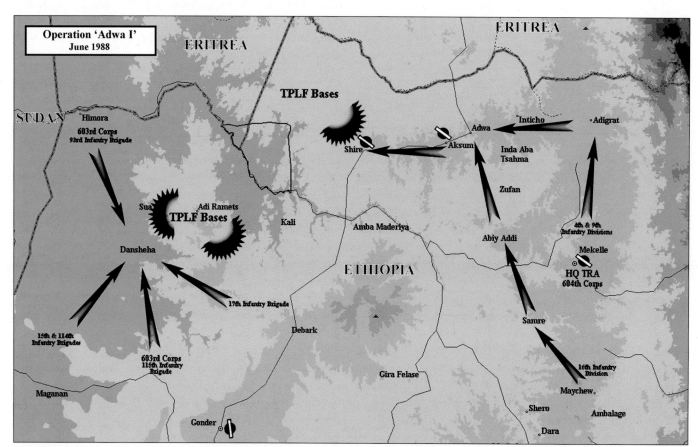

Map 1 Reconstruction of major directions of the Ethiopian advance during Operation Adwa (later 'Adwa I') in June 1988. (Map by Tom Cooper)

another pair of helicopters, about one hour later. Then, at 1130 hrs, two MiGs released the first bombs directly over the market: as people tried to escape in panic, they were cut down by machine-gun fire from two helicopters. Another pair of helicopters and MiGs repeated this exercise – consisting of bombardment followed by multiple strafing runs – about half an hour later. Indeed, the procedure was continued the entire day until 1830 hrs local time: each new wave hit Hausien just as the people came out of where they attempted to shelter and started recovering the injured. The town was left shrouded in a thick cloud of smoke that by noon had turned the day into night: dozens of homes were bombed out or burned, together with hundreds of people that attempted to find shelter inside.

The exact number of victims of the massacre in Hausien remains unknown today; not only because the task of recovering the dead from the rubble was incomplete even one month later, or because the EtAF simultaneously hit multiple towns and villages nearby, but also because many of those killed came from far away and thus it was impossible to precisely identify them. For example, a pair of Mi-24s or Mi-35s attacked the market of Abyi Addi the same day. Furthermore, due to poor medical facilities, hundreds of the wounded succumbed to their injuries during the following days. Eventually, almost every single village in the Hausien area reported between 40 and 80 killed on 22 June 1988.[21] Smaller air strikes had targeted Enticho, Mai Kenetal, and Atsbi, during the following days, killing more than 50 in total. Reacting in a rather grotesque fashion, Addis Ababa first strenuously denied any of the crimes in question, then explained that its pilots mistook people gathering at the market in Hausien for insurgents, while ignoring all the other attacks.[22] In comparison, when interviewed about such operations while still in captivity of the EPLF, Major Bezabih Petros, left no doubts:

'We definitely know civilians will get hurt. But, knowing that the people sympathise with the rebels, the order is to bomb everything that moves.'[23]

About a dozen Mil Mi-35 helicopter gunships were acquired by Ethiopia starting in 1984. Shown is the example with the serial number 2105. In 1988-1991, they were often deployed for attacks on civilian populations in insurgent-controlled parts of Eritrea and Tigray, with often tragic consequences for those on the receiving end. (Herve Dessallier via Albert Grandolini)

The MiG-23BN – this photograph shows the example with serial number 1270 – remained one of the primary platforms for attacks on civilians in insurgent-controlled areas in the 1988-1991 period. (Herve Dessallier via Albert Grandolini)

Adwa II: On the Verge of Triumph

One of the primary reasons for TPLF's weak resistance to the advance of the 604th Corps, was the insurgents' decision to concentrate most of their forces to face the 603rd Corps in Gondar. The Ethiopian offensive in this area began on 19 June, when units of the 603rd Corps opened an advance on Dansha from multiple directions. Once secured, the town was used as the launching point against the primary base of the TPLF, scheduled to start in coordination with the second phase of 604th Corps' operations.

With departure points of the 603rd Corps being closer to the TPLF's bases, this advance met stronger resistance. Indeed, the 15th and 114th Infantry Brigades came forward so slowly that Colonel Bekele Haile, commander of their parent 7th Infantry Division, was arrested and dismissed. Meanwhile, the 115th, 33rd, and 17th Infantry Brigades advanced from Tikil Dingai, Humera and Dabaraq, respectively, with the later facing particularly bitter resistance in Addi Arqay.

The TPLF was not the only one to slow down the 603rd Corps: terrain – which included hills covered by trees and intersected by multiple rivers – proved unusually difficult, and most of the involved units had to make use of horses to carry their supplies because motorised vehicles proved useless. Therefore their firepower was limited too, because they could not take their tanks nor artillery with them, but only mortars. Indeed, the 33rd Infantry Brigade, which had the advantage of advancing along the road linking Humera with Gondar, was forced to slow down in order to let the others to catch up and avoid becoming isolated. Despite all the difficulties, the 603rd Corps finally reached Dansha, on 28 June 1988, and quickly captured the town.

At this point in time, a debate erupted in the Ethiopian High Command over the issue of what to do next, and where. The commander of the TRA and officers from the Ministry of Defence advised a halt to the operation until the end of the rainy season, and then delivering the blow against the main TPLF base under better conditions. Furthermore, they expected the exhausted troops to rest, and their stocks of supplies to be replenished by then. However, Captain Asfaw overruled all the professional officers and ordered the further advance – Operation Adwa II – to be re-launched without any further delay.

Therefore, the 603rd and 604th Corps opened the assault on the TPLF's main base, protected by four brigades, supported by several T-55s and a few anti-aircraft cannons, on 3 July 1988. Although encountering bitter resistance, they managed to break through and take the training camp in Kaza, before entering Dejena, thus coming very close to their ultimate target. However, the 4th and 9th Divisions of the 604th Corps were meanwhile delayed by atrocious, muddy terrain separating Shire from the Takese River, where most of their vehicles became bogged down. This enabled the insurgents to further slow down these two divisions with help of merely a thin protective screen, while concentrating most of their troops against the 603rd Corps. To add salt to the injury, at this crucial moment in time, the weather turned for the worse and made EtAF support for ground troops – most of whom were meanwhile hopelessly exhausted – impossible.

On 9 July 1988, the TPLF initiated its counter-attack on the 603rd Corps, forcing its units to withdraw towards Dansha. Indeed, under the cover of the rain and fog, the insurgents then assaulted Dansha, in turn causing a complete collapse of the Ethiopian Army's corps: its units fell back in chaos towards Humara and Gondar, leaving 4,426 casualties in their trail, of which more than 2,000 were inflicted in the last few days alone.

Immediately afterwards, the TPLF crossed the Tekeze River and assaulted the 604th Corps. On 15 July, the Tigrayans outmanoeuvred the 4th and 9th Infantry Divisions, and hit their rear, forcing them into a retreat towards Shire, which they reached three days later.[24]

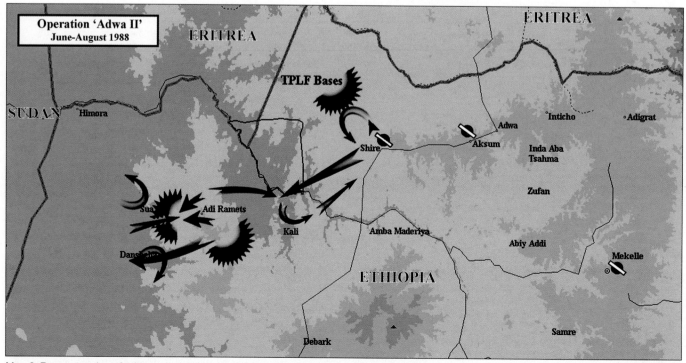

Map 2 Reconstruction of primary directions of major Ethiopian units during Operation Adwa II. (Map by Tom Cooper)

The last stage of this battle took place two weeks later. Although barely surviving a major setback, the 604th Corps was ordered to launch a new offensive, this time through deploying the 4th, 9th and 16th Infantry Divisions along the road from Shire to Badme, with the intention of destroying all insurgent bases in the Sheraro area. The three units left Shire on 29 July. Although repeatedly ambushed, they punched through until reaching the vicinity of their objective. Sensing an opportunity, the TPLF meanwhile concentrated the major part of its regular brigades on this frontline and then, under cover of bad weather, launched Operation Hausien on 3 August 1988. Its first blow left the 22nd and 120th Infantry Brigades isolated from the neighbouring 75th and 128th Infantry Brigades. The encircled brigades were then forced to fight for naked survival, without any kind of help. Major-General Mulatu Negash later recalled:

'We fought for three days without air support. It was a battle of bombs and hand grenades. Our losses were unprecedented. For lack of reserves, victory was snatched from our hands...'

Ultimately, the 604th Corps suffered such casualties that it could not but fall back towards Shire on 11 August. Surprisingly enough, the CO of the TRA still considered Operation Adwa a success – because he assessed that the TPLF was decimated.[25]

Operations Aksum and Degen

After two months of intensive operations, and defeats of July and August 1988, the 604th Corps was sorely in need of rest and refit, and remained on the defensive in the Shire area for the rest of the year. However, contrary to the assessments of Ethiopian commanders, the TPLF was still in good shape. Indeed, close to its bases and a network of parallel roads it had constructed in the area, it quickly severed the logistic routes of the Ethiopian corps. Furthermore, the road connecting Shire with Gondar was made impassable when the insurgents blew up the bridge over the Tekeze River, while the road connecting Shire with Adwa was subjected to such a series of ambushes, that it became much too dangerous for the movement of supply convoys. Indeed, when the TPLF then recaptured Aksum in one of its counterattacks, the survival of the 604th Corps depended exclusively on the EtAF's ability to keep it supplied. Preferring to spend the time with reorganization and expansion of their regular forces – which were subsequently grouped into seven divisions of about 3,600 officers and other ranks each – the insurgents did not attempt to deliver a coup de main. The isolated corps thus received the opportunity to expand the airstrip at Shire enough to enable landings of fully-loaded An-12s. Nevertheless, because the EtAF lacked enough transport aircraft to keep it properly supplied, and was also busy elsewhere, the 604th remained a major burden, and on a logistical shoestring, under a constant threat of shortages of food and ammunition. It is hardly necessary to say that this resulted in constantly increasing rates of desertions.[26]

Searching for a way out of this situation, the Chief of Operations at the Ministry of National Defence (MOND) in Addis Ababa, Major-General Demissie Bulto, proposed a new offensive, this time with cooperation between the TRA and the SRA, and with the aim of re-opening the road from Asmara via Adwa to Shire. In accordance with his ideas, the SRA's 10th Infantry Division would advance from Eritrea and take Rama, while the 9th and 16th Infantry Divisions of the 604th Corps would advance from Selekleka and Shire in the opposite direction. In this fashion, he hoped to sandwich a large portion of TPLF forces detected in between. Essentially, Bulto's idea was accepted. However, while the planning of what became Operation Aksum I, the TRA's headquarters opted to assign a separate axis of advance to two of its divisions, and left the 4th Infantry at Shire, instead of grouping them all in a single and less vulnerable body, as advised by the MOND.

This offensive was opened early in the morning of 28 December 1988, with the 9th Infantry Division advancing along the road from Axum to Shire, while the 16th Infantry Division moved northwards. Soon, the two units were separated from each other by between 10 and 15 kilometres. Unsurprisingly considering its excellent intelligence, the TPLF seized the opportunity to beat the opponent in detail. After concentrating some six brigades and two heavy-weapons battalions, it assaulted the 16th Infantry Division at the moment its vanguard – the 128th Infantry Brigade – became isolated from the rest of formation because of its rapid progress. On 29 December 1988, the insurgents encircled the unfortunate brigade and mauled it, killing its commanding officer. Immediately afterwards, the TPLF re-oriented its units against the rest of the 16th Infantry Division, and subjected it to such a series of attacks that it fell back on Selekleka by 30 December. Following this reverse, the headquarters of the 604th Corps requested an end to the entire operation. Surprisingly enough, Major-General Multau Negash refused.

Correspondingly, the TPLF was left free to force-march towards the 9th Infantry Division and deploy two of its brigades undetected around its flanks before attacking from three sides. The brunt of this assault fell upon the 110th Infantry Brigade, which suffered correspondingly. The nearby 75th Infantry Brigade fell back at first, followed by the whole division, but the flow of this battle turned when the 22nd and the 120th Infantry Brigades of the 16th Infantry Division arrived on the scene and launched a hasty counterattack – this time supported by helicopter gunships and several air strikes of the EtAF. This proved only a temporary relief: by 31 December 1988, all of the involved Ethiopian units were back at Selekleka, with the 9th Infantry Division having lost one third of its troops in a matter of just a few days. Unsurprisingly, the 10th Infantry Division never managed to breach the TPLF's defences in the Rama area, and thus its attempt to distract the insurgents failed too.[27]

Bombing Everything that Moves

During the second half of 1988, the commanders of the EtAF had apparently concluded that air strikes on towns and villages controlled by the insurgents were getting ever less effective. The primary reason was that due to the activity of the air force by day, and despite incredible problems this was causing, most local markets were held by the night. Correspondingly, the Ethiopian Air Force began targeting the production of food in areas controlled by the insurgents instead – i.e. farmers that worked their fields. Additional targets included the livestock and trains of camels and mules carrying food and supplies – whether for the insurgents or for the local population.

In September 1988, the EtAF concentrated on bombing villages in the Barka region of Eritrea, while in the following month it repeatedly bombed Agordat, and its MiG-23ML interceptors even attempted to attack two locust-spraying aircraft inside the Sudanese airspace. The marketplace of Chilla, one of REST's main locations for distributing famine relief, was hit by at least five air strikes in November 1988. By the end of the year, it became impossible to move any livestock or vehicles during daylight hours in most of Eritrea and Tigray. Over 100,000 civilians were displaced, of whom about 40,000 fled to Sudan.[28]

Bolstering Failure: Aksum II

Determined to continue in the same style, the headquarters of the TRA requested reinforcements – and the MOND was more than pleased to serve. During the following days, An-12s of the EtAF flew at least 2,400 newly-trained conscripts to Shire, to bolster depleted units, and then the entire 103rd Commando Division too. However, upon its arrival, the 103rd was found as ill-suited for anything more than to garrison Mekelle.[29] The resulting void was filled with the 6th and 30th Mechanised Brigades, brought in from Wello Province, and the 17th Infantry Division from Gondar. Their further preparations were not only more closely supervised by the leadership of the TRA – which established its forward headquarters in Shire – but also by the presence of Major-General Negash and Captain Asfaw.

Of course, the TPLF quickly found out about this re-deployment and on 1 February 1989 launched Operation Degen, targeting the 603rd Corps' units deployed along the road from Gondar to Shire. The first insurgent attack hit the garrison of Dabat. When the 133rd Infantry Brigade was rushed in to relieve, it ran into an ambush and was mauled. Meanwhile, the insurgents overwhelmed the string of checkpoints along the road, and finally overran the 136th Infantry Brigade that defended Debrak, where they found a huge – and perfectly intact – ammunition depot. Isolated, the garrison of Dabat was forced to retreat towards Gondar: on the way there, it was ambushed too.[30]

Undeterred, the TRA opened Operation Aksum II. This time, the 103rd Commando Division was ordered to advance from Mekelle to Aksum, followed by the 9th Infantry Division. The 16th Infantry Division was to secure their rear, while the 4th Infantry Division was to garrison Shire. Once it reached Aksum, the 103rd let the 9th Infantry pass by and take the lead while advancing in the direction of Adwa. In this fashion, the Ethiopians avoided the mistake of advancing along separate axes. However, this time their intelligence made a gross mistake by under-evaluating the strength of the TPLF: instead of three, this deployed five full divisions.

On 8 February 1989, the 604th Corps left Selekleka to start two days of flawless advance in the face of no resistance at all. Ignoring the fact that they were advancing ever deeper into a trap, the Ethiopians continued until the 1035th Brigade of the 103rd Commando Division crashed headlong into a major TPLF position a few kilometres short of Aksum. In the course of a confused battle, one of its battalions lost the way and was completely destroyed. Meanwhile, the mass of insurgent units was carefully hiding on both flanks of this advance and thus avoided the detection by the army's scouts. They launched their

counterattack early in the morning of 10 February 1989 by simultaneously attacking the rear-guard and the flanks of the Ethiopian force. The 22nd Infantry Brigade of the 16th Infantry Division, which was holding the vital peak of May Brazio near Selekleka, was subjected to relentless attacks, while the light infantry of the TPLF systematically manoeuvred around its flanks, mortaring and machine-gunning as it went. Despite intensive support of Mi-24/35s and EtAF MiG-23BNs, and the courageous and fierce resistance of the 22nd Infantry Brigade, the Ethiopian command structure then completely collapsed. By 1045, the headquarters of the 604th Corps felt forced to order the 103rd Commando Division to withdraw. In the ensuing confusion, the 1035th Brigade was delayed, and found itself isolated. A mere 450 of its 1,200 officers and other ranks managed it back to Selekleka. Pursuing the retreating enemy, the insurgents secured the May Brazio, late in the morning, thus isolating elements from no less than three Ethiopian Army's divisions. The 75th Infantry Brigade from the 16th Infantry Division and the 142nd Infantry Brigade of the 9th Infantry Division were nearly destroyed in the process, while the motorised element of the 103rd Commando Brigade ran into a textbook ambush that simultaneously hit the front and the rear of its column. Groups of survivors continued fleeing in the direction of Selekleka through most of 11 February 1989.[31]

The End of the 604th Corps

After the disaster of Operation Aksum II, most of the 604th Corps was a hollow shell. With only 7,300 troops between them, the 4th, 9th, and 16th Infantry Divisions, and the 103rd Commando Division, were struggling to secure at least Selekleka and Shire. Casualties amongst their officers were so severe, that most of the companies were led by mere privates without any kind of specialist training. Unsurprisingly, morale was at rock bottom, especially militiamen feeling betrayed and forced to serve after the end of their service term. In best shape was the 4th Infantry Division, which still had about 5,000 troops, including many seasoned veterans of the Ogaden War.[32]

Realising the enemy could not hold both towns – separated by about 30 kilometres – the TPLF decided to quickly reorganize and replenish its forces in this area and then launch a new offensive, Operation Hawzien II. Correspondingly, the insurgents hurriedly prepared for another battle. During this time, they greatly benefitted from resumption of military cooperation with the EPLF: indeed, the EPLA deployed its 19th Brigade of the 52nd Division into the area. This was a significant contribution because that unit was a combined-arms formation, supported by 12 MBTs, 8 field guns, and a dozen ZU-23 anti-aircraft cannons. Overall composition of the forces involved in the following battles is provided in Tables 4 and 5.

As usual, the TPLF sought to beat the enemy in detail, and thus first concentrated most of its forces against Salaklaka. The assault was opened at dawn of 15 February 1989 by the insurgent infantry exploiting numerous gaps between major Ethiopian positions. In this fashion, they quickly seized several ridges surrounding the town, including the towering Mount Qoyasa, which was used to emplace artillery pieces. Meanwhile, another insurgent force dislodged the 120th Brigade from the high ground overseeing the Afghagah Pass on the road connecting Salaklaka and Shire, thus de-facto encircling the 9th and 16th Infantry Divisions. Both Ethiopian units attempted, desperately, to force their way out, but suffered extensive losses in the process. One of the survivors recalled:

'The land was strewn with the dead and wounded. All attempts at breaking in force failed. Everyone was looking for an exit from the hellish place. I was one of those who made it.'

Although numerous survivors eventually did manage to reach Shire, both the 9th and 16th Infantry Divisions were virtually destroyed: sad remnants of the latter were subsequently put under the command of the commander of the local detachment of the military police. However, the TPLF delivered its next blow long before the officers of the 604th Corps ever had a serious chance of reorganizing their mauled units again. Superior in numbers and fire-power, they assaulted positions of the 4th Infantry Division protecting Shire from north and north-east at 0200 hrs of 18 February 1989. This blow came as a shock even to seasoned Ethiopian veterans, because they had never before found themselves on the receiving end of a comparable artillery barrage and infantry assaults. Certainly enough, the 4th Infantry held out and even repulsed an assault by the EPLA's 19th Brigade, between 1100 and 1200 hrs, destroying several Eritrean tanks in the process. However, in the meantime the 103rd Commando Division began breaking apart and fell back towards the local airport, followed by survivors from the 9th and 16th Infantry Divisions.

Reacting to the collapse of the enemy, the insurgent commanders then changed their plan: they re-deployed the Aurora and Alula Division around the enemy flanks and began assaulting the hodgepodge, consisting of survivors from the 9th, 16th and 103rd Divisions, at the airport instead of the well-entrenched 4th Infantry Division. Despite desperate calls from their officers, the troops refused to fight. Major-General Negash then fled on board one of the EtAF's transports – allegedly to call for reinforcements – leaving the 604th Corps to its own fate. Leaning back on the fact that the 111th Brigade of the 4th Infantry was still holding its positions, the remaining Ethiopian officers issued the order to blow up and burn all the supply depots, and then formed a huge convoy, including more than 200 trucks, which moved out along the road for Gondar. However, the TPLF had meanwhile deployed a blocking force to Endabaguna, and this ambushed

Table 4: TPLF Order of Battle, Operation Hawzien II, February 1989

Units	Commanders	Notes
Overall commanders	Hayelom Araya Abebe Tekle Haimanot Samora Yunus	
Agazi Division		
Alula Division	CO Saare Makonen Yimer	
Aurora Division	CO Yohannes Gebremesqel	
May Day Division		
Yekatit Division		
19th Brigade		from 52nd Division EPLA

Table 5: TRA Order of Battle, February 1989

Unit	Commander	Notes
604th Corps (HQ Shire)	Major-General Mulatu Negash Brigadier-General Addis Agilachew	
4th Infantry Division	Colonel Kebede Biru	including 111th and 138th Infantry Brigades
9th Infantry Division		75th, 110th, 142nd Infantry Brigades
16th Infantry Division	Colonel Berhanu Woldegiorgis	22nd, 120th, 128th, 135th Infantry Brigades
103rd Commando Division	Colonel Getahun Gebregioris	including 1035th Commando Brigade

the Ethiopians, killing hundreds. Whatever was still intact of the 604th Corps by that moment in time, ceased to exist by 1900 hrs of 18 February 1989. Over the following months, about 6,000 Ethiopian survivors managed to reach friendly positions, usually following a harrowing flight through the TPLF-controlled territory, while having to evade even the local population which was fiercely anti-Derg.[33]

Following the patterns established by the EPLA, by 1988 the TPLF was operating its first 'heavy' units, including mechanised and motorised elements. The majority of vehicles included diverse trucks of Soviet and East European origin captured from the Ethiopian army. (Adrien Fontanellaz Collection)

A still from a video showing one of the EPLA's first 'heavy' units, equipped with T-54/55 MBTs captured from the Ethiopian Army. (EPLF)

Victorious insurgents atop a so-called 'technical': a truck mounting a twin-barrel ZU-23 anti-aircraft cannon (calibre 23mm), captured from the Ethiopian Army. (Mark Lepko Collection)

Leaving Tigray Forever

Behind the withdrawing military, the TPLF collected a rich booty, including at least one operational BM-21 multiple rocket launcher system (MRLS), 11 T-54 and T-55s, and 11 D-30 howitzers. Two other tanks, a pair of BM-21s, and nine D-30s had been destroyed. Most importantly, the loss of the TRA's most powerful corps shocked and panicked the Derg and the MOND, prompting them into decisions that were to have tremendous effects upon the subsequent flow of this war.

Late on 18 February 1989, the MOND issued the order for all Ethiopian Army units to withdraw from Adigrat. A few days later, a similar decision was taken in regards of Humera. The destruction of the 604th Corps thus nullified the progress made at such a high cost during Operation Adwa. However, even worse was to follow: on 27 February, the MOND came to the decision to withdraw all of its forces from Tigray. Correspondingly,

a huge convoy carrying about 24,000 troops and thousands of government officials and their families left Mekelle. In their wake, the Ethiopians destroyed all the important installations and government buildings, including extensive depots fully stocked with ammunition and supplies. The Derg thus gave up all hopes of ever again establishing direct land communication between Addis Ababa and Asmara. Henceforth, the SRA could only be kept resupplied via the road connecting the capital with the port of Asseb, from where everything had to be shipped to Massawa. Worse yet, the other main logistical artery – the air-bridge to Asmara – was also impacted because the loss of Mekelle meant the loss of the local airport too. In turn, the duration of flights by transport aircraft to Asmara more than doubled. By 4 March 1989, the insurgents thus found themselves in total control of the province – although the TPLF remained cautious not to enter Mekelle for three days longer.[34]

CHAPTER 3
LOOMING DISASTER

With the war going on for years without the prospect of a victory or other lasting solutions, and confronted with Mengistu Haile Mariam's dictatorship, a number of high-ranking officers of the Ethiopian military concluded that there was no other way but to topple the government. Their plot was set in motion in mid-May 1989, during the strongman's visit to East Germany. The coup failed, resulting in the arrest and death of nearly all of the plotters. In their place, Mengistu positioned less-competent, but politically reliable favourites, thus strengthening his grip on the armed forces better than ever before. However, he never appointed a new minister of defence again, and actually scored a pyrrhic victory. Not only that his survival further fragmentised the core essence of the survival of his regime – the Ethiopian military – but afterwards the dissatisfaction within the officer corps reached such proportions, that some of these began leaking sensitive intelligence and plans for operations to the insurgents in a hope this might hasten the fall of the Derg.

The Coup in Addis Ababa

At first glance, the Derg had no serious chance of withstanding a coup attempt because the plotters included top officers of all branches, foremost Major-General Haile Gebremikael (Chief-of-Staff Army), Major-General Amha Desta (Chief-of-Staff EtAF), and Rear-Admiral Tesfaye Berhanu (Chief-of-Staff Navy). Even prestigious Major-General Fanta Belay (former Chief-of-Staff EtAF and meanwhile the Minister of Industry) and Major-General Demissie Bulto, commander of the SRA, became involved, together with dozens of other officers, foremost from the air force. However, their plan was extremely hazardous: due to the complex, tripartite system of command, none of the plotters could exercise direct control of any significant military and police units in the capital. Furthermore, the only military force garrisoned in Addis Ababa was the Special Defence Brigade (SDB), a crack unit of Derg-loyalists commanded by Brigadier-General Garramaw Baqqala. In essence, the SDB

was a sort of Praetorian Guard for Mengistu and, totalling more than 10,000 well-trained troops supported by armour, it possessed fighting power several times greater than any of the army's divisions. Correspondingly, the plotters depended on their ability to mobilise reinforcements from garrisons outside Addis Ababa.

The coup was set in motion during a meeting of top officers of the MOND in the Armed Forces Building, early on the morning of 18 May 1989. Simultaneously, two MiG-23BNs from Debre Zeit AB flew several passes at low altitude above Addis Ababa. However, the Minister of Defence, Major-General Hailegiorgis Habtemaraim, not only remained loyal but was informed about the plot. He went to the Armed Forces Building and entered negotiations with plotters, attempting to convince them to give up their attempt. During the ensuing exchange, Habtemariam was shot and killed.

This bought the time for the SDB to move out, secure all the important buildings around Addis Ababa and surround the Armed Forces Building. Finding out about the air force's involvement and planning for An-12 transports to bring a force of 513 troops from the SRA to Debre Zeit air base, while helicopters would transport a company from the Camp Tatek-2, Baggala meanwhile ordered diverse elements of the SDB into action outside the city. One column secured Debre Zeit, despite threats from the local commander to deploy an Antonov to bomb the Presidential Palace. Indeed, when the dissident soldiers from the SRA landed at Debre Zeit, at 1700hrs, they were all arrested on the spot. Similarly, when helicopters deployed the contingent from Tatek-2 at the old airport of Addis Ababa, they were quickly neutralised by the SDB in the course of a short fight. Realising that their attempt was failing, most of the officers in the Armed Forces Building then surrendered to the loyalists: only a handful managed to escape through the cordon, while Major-Generals Amha Desta and Merid Negussie committed suicide. The coup in Addis Ababa was thus quelled within only 15 hours.

Major-General Amha Desta meeting a Soviet delegation in Addis Ababa. (EtAF via S. N.)

A soldier of the SDB or the 102nd Airborne Division (recognizable by their maroon-coloured barrettes), on the streets of Addis Ababa in 1988. (Adrien Fontanellaz Collection)

Troops of the 102nd Airborne Division underway in a truck down a street of Asmara, following the coup attempt of 18 May 1989. (Adiren Fontanellaz Collection)

Mutiny in Asmara

In the meantime, dissident troops of the SRA took control of most of the military bases in Eritrea. However – and although supported by the commanders of the 2nd Infantry Division in that city, of the 3rd Infantry Division in Keren, and the 6th Infantry Division in Massawa, as well as the commanders of the Air and Navy Bases in Massawa – Major-General Demissie Bulto was far from being in total control. Indeed, officers that sided with him proved incapable of taking decisive steps against the Derg. They merely deployed one An-12 to drop leaflets over the capital. On the contrary, as soon as he was back in Ethiopia, Mengistu was able to contact loyalists and coordinate a counter-coup with them, spearheaded by the 102nd Airborne Division. Not only that this unit had already earned itself a ruthless reputation: most of its officers were convinced that the principal reason for lack of success and heavy Ethiopian losses in the war was because of sabotage by high-ranking officers that opposed the Derg. Now, they were given clear targets. Troops of the 102nd quickly overran the Kagnew base, where they killed Major-General Bulto. Other elements secured the Asmara AB, where they gravely injured Brigadier-General Neguse Zagraw (commander of the 2nd Command, EtAF). During the following week, they brought all other major headquarters and military bases under their control and launched a wave of brutal repression. Top coup-plotters were summarily executed and their beheaded bodies dragged behind trucks in the streets of Asmara. On 7 June 1989, Mengistu himself announced that 146 high-ranking officers had been arrested and 27 of them – including 11 generals – executed in that city alone. Further executions followed nearly a year later: 12 high-ranking officers were executed on 20 May 1990.[35]

Birth of the EPRDF

In the meantime, as soon as it was in full control of Tigray, and while preparing for large-scale operations in other provinces, the TPLF launched a campaign of formalising it status and relations to multiple other insurgent formations. Thus came into being the Ethiopian People's Revolutionary Democratic Front (EPRDF). Over time, and except for the TPLF, this front was to include such groups as the Ethiopian People's Democratic Movement (EPDM), Ethiopian Democratic Officers' Revolutionary Movement (EDORM), The Oromo People's Democratic Organisation (OPDO), and the Afar Democratic Union (ADU), but also Sudanese proxies like Bani Shangul People's Liberation front (BPLF), with about 1,500 combatants, and the Gambela People's Democratic Front (GPDF), with about 1,200 combatants, created by Khartoum with the aim of fighting the SPLA in Ethiopia proper. Essentially, the resulting 'Front' was a classic Maoist political-military body ensuring that – while retaining the control over the battlefield, the TPLF could gain popular support from other people by not being perceived as strictly Tigrayan. Correspondingly, it was chaired by Meles Zenawi, TPLF's leader, and four of the seven members of its Executive Committee were from his organisation too.[36]

Israeli Deal

The EtAF had shown significant discontent with the Derg and thus a number of its pilots defected to Yemen and Sudan after the failure of the coup. The government thus subjected the air force to a careful screening before authorising its transport units to operate again, starting on 23 May 1989. One of the results was that the 3rd Command at Dire Dawa AB was effectively disbanded: subsequently, all the basic training of future EtAF pilots was handled by the Pilot Training School (PTS) of the Ethiopian Airlines at Bole International Airport. Similarly, all basic training of future ground personnel was henceforth run by the Mechanic Training School (MTC) of the Ethiopian Airlines.[37]

Nevertheless, the air force continued its campaign of counter-value raids – before and after the coup. In March 1989, its fighter bombers repeatedly bombed Shire, Humera, Adwa and Axum in Tigray, killing several dozens. On 30 March 1989, the EtAF bombed the ancient church of St Mary of Zion in Axum: a famous site of pilgrimage and a cultural relic of great historic importance in a town considered a holy place by many Ethiopian Christians. Three civilians were killed, and the church – located in the main section of the town, adjacent to a museum and another church – was badly damaged. Often reported in the international media, and followed by the unsuccessful coup attempt, such attacks resulted in the Derg regime becoming isolated on the diplomatic level. By 1988, even Moscow began exercising pressure for Mengistu to open negotiations with the armed opposition, while Cuba announced its intention to withdraw remaining troops by the end of the following year.[38]

In reaction to the Soviet pressure, the Derg opened talks with the EPLF. These were held under the mediation of the former US President Jimmy Carter in Atlanta, Nairobi and Washington, between September 1989 and February 1991. Furthermore, the Derg negotiated with the EPRDF in Rome, in November and December 1989, and in March 1990. However, the insurgents quickly understood that this was little other than a show, and an attempt to blame them as the party responsible for continuation of the war. On the contrary: perfectly aware of the fact that the Derg regime was rather fragile, the negotiations only made them determined to end the conflict with a clear-cut victory.[39]

Meanwhile, facing receding support from Eastern Europe, Addis Ababa began turning to North Korea and Israel with requests for help. Although Pyongyang proved willing to provide advisors and material support it was no viable alternative to the USSR: as of 1989,

not only did it not possess the necessary industrial capabilities, but most of the armament it was able to sell was of even lesser quality than that provided by the Soviets. Nevertheless, small batches of tanks and self-propelled artillery pieces were acquired during the year, and North Korean instructors started training a number of new, specialised units of the Ethiopian Army.

Relations between the Derg and Tel Aviv were originally established in 1983, when Israel delivered ammunition of Soviet origin – captured in Lebanon – worth US$ 20 million. This cooperation further intensified a year later, when the Derg permitted the Israelis to evacuate about 10,000 Falashas – or Beita Israel, members of the Jewish community living in Ethiopia for centuries – via Sudan, within the frame of Operation Moses. On 17 September 1989, Israel opened its embassy in Addis Ababa, and the two governments almost instantly reached another agreement for evacuation of additional Falashas by 1991 (Operation Solomon), in exchange for delivery of arms – including Israeli-made CBUs – and military-related supplies to Ethiopia. Correspondingly, Israel delivered four patrol boats to the Ethiopian Navy, while its advisors began training the Ethiopian intelligence services and the SDB.[40]

Delivered despite consistent opposition from the US government, the first consignment of about 100 Israeli-made CBUs was deployed by the EtAF by September 1989, when it bombed civilians in Takeze Bridge, Chercher, Gobye, Raya, Kulmelsk, and Axum in Tigray, killing dozens. The next month, the MiGs bombed Mekelle at least twice, killing more than 50, while in November 1989, it hit Adwa and Zalambesa in Tigray, Kara Mishig in Shewa, Tenta in Wollo and Degollo on the Wollo-Shewa border.[41]

A group of EtAF MiG-21bis pilots with one of their mounts inside a hardened aircraft shelter at Asmara Airport in the late 1980s. (EtAF via S.N.)

A view of Asmara Airport (and Air Base), from the mid-1980s. Visible are, amongst others, eight MiG-23BNs and five MiG-21s – all assigned to the 2nd Command of EtAF. Asmara was the base from which most attacks on civilians within areas controlled by EPLF's and TPLF's insurgencies were launched. (Pit Weinert Collection)

Peace Through Struggle

Of course, following its withdrawal from Tigray and the failed coup, the Derg reorganised its army, too. Amongst others, the 605th Corps was re-positioned to protect the Wello Province, with its 1st Infantry Division deployed in Maychew, the 17th Infantry in Korem, the 27th Infantry in Alamata, and the 6th Mechanised Brigade in Kobo. This area became the primary target of the next TPLF offensive, Operation Selam ba Tigil ('Peace Through Struggle'), in the course of which the Front for the first time deployed a combination of its own heavy arms units and light infantry.

For Operation Peace Through Struggle, the TPLF grouped its units into two: commanded by Hayelom Araya, one group was to attack Maychew and Korem, while the other, commanded by Samora Yunus, advanced from Mekelle across the Afar lowlands and thus around the Ethiopian flank before cutting the Mekelle-Dessie road at Dore Geber, near the critical crossroad of Woldya, thus threatening to isolate the 605th Corps from the headquarters and supply dumps of the TRA in Dessie.

The operation proved a success right from the start, on 20 August 1989. Under pressure, the 1st and 17th Infantry Division quickly withdrew to Alamata. Instead of attacking this town, the insurgents bypassed it and set up an ambush at the Cube Bar Pass, on the road to Kobo. This prompted the 605th Corps to hurriedly evacuate all three of its divisions to Kobo, leaving behind not only their wounded, but also plenty of supplies. Even then, the troops still had to force their way through the blocked pass, suffering heavy casualties.

All three divisions of the 605th Corps were regrouped in Kobo by 31 August, when the TPLF opened its attack on that town. During the following nine days, EtAF fighter-bombers and helicopter gunships of the Army Aviation Battalion flew 248 combat sorties against insurgents, significantly contributing to the successful defence of Kobo. Nevertheless, the TPLF's defence was fierce, and at least one MiG-21, one MiG-23BN and four helicopters were damaged by ground fire.

In the meantime, the MOND ordered the SRA to reinforce the TRA through re-deploying the 5th and 8th Brigades of the 102nd Airborne Division to Woldya. From there, the two units advanced along the road to Kobo. However, on 3 September 1989, they were ambushed by a second TPLF force, which had entrenched itself in Doro Geber, and lost Colonel Getahun Kefle, Commander of the 102nd Airborne Division. Unsurprisingly, the morale of the 605th Corps was, meanwhile, shattered. The 140th Infantry Brigade abandoned its positions without corresponding orders and despite officers opening fire with ZU-23 anti-aircraft cannon at their own troops.[42] On the contrary, even the officers of the forward headquarters of the TRA and the 605th Corps had lost their nerves and ordered their evacuation to Woldya. This decision broke the back of all the troops; although most of units were still perfectly intact, the entire corps fell back in the same direction, falling apart in the process.[43] Eventually, most of the 605th Corps did manage to break through at Doro Geber and reach Woldya, but not before clashing with a force that was advancing from the town in their direction – which proved to be the 26th Infantry Division: at least three T-55s were destroyed in this 'blue-on-blue'

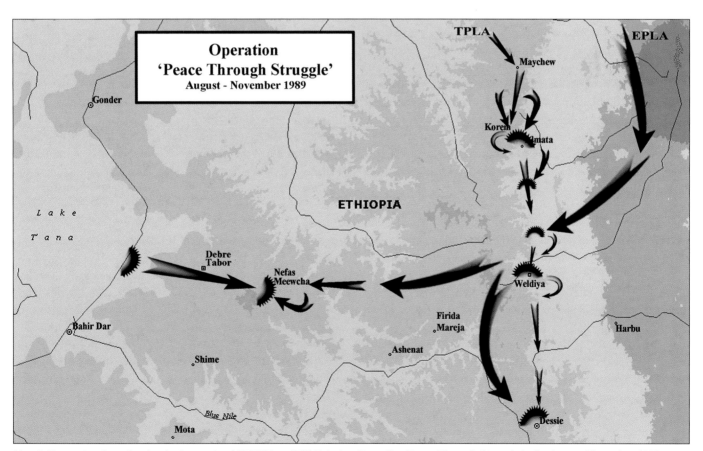

Map 3 Reconstruction of major deployments of EPRDF and TPLF during Operation Peace Through Struggle in the August-November 1989 period. Repeatedly outflanking and setting up blocking positions in their rear areas, caused an outright collapse of the involved Ethiopian Army units. (Map by Tom Cooper)

engagement. Despite widespread chaos, the TRA still managed to reconstitute most of its units and build-up a cohesive defence line around Woldya. This was protected by the 17th and 27th Infantry Divisions, the 5th and 8th Airborne Brigades, and the 30th Mechanised Brigade – all of which were reorganised just in time to repulse the first TLPF assault on the town launched on 11 September 1989.

EPRDF's Blitzkrieg

The EPRDF launched several additional attacks on Woldya by 7 October 1989, all of which remained unsuccessful – before reaching the decision to overcome the stalemate by resuming manoeuvre warfare, in which it exceled.[44] Leaving behind just a token force to tie down an entire corps of the Ethiopian Army, it continued its advance with another two-prong offensive. The Aurora Division marched along the road to Werata, entering the Gondar Province and hitting directly into the rear of the 603rd Corps, the primary units of which were still holding positions facing Tigray. The Aurora Division quickly overran the garrison of Debre Zebit, and entrenched itself there. Underestimating the threat to his rear, the Ethiopian Corps-commander, Brigadier-General Abbaba Hayle Selasse, launched a brigade-sized counterattack, but this was easily repulsed. On the contrary, the insurgents then invested Nefas Meechwa, and beat back a counterattack of the 25th Infantry Brigade (supported by a battery of BM-21 MRLS). The latter fell back towards the next locality along the same road, Kimir Dengay, garrisoned by the 18th Infantry Brigade. Only there – and after the 603rd Corps reinforced its two brigades by a third formation of this size, the 33rd Infantry – were the Ethiopians finally able to block the further advance of the Aurora Division.

The target of the second pincer of the EPRDF's advance was Dessie. In order to take this town, the Front deployed no less than three of its divisions: the TPLF's Agazi and Qy Kokab, and the EPLDM's Lab Adar. Initially, these formations advanced through the mountains parallel to the main road, before turning to approach their target, on 11 October 1989. Before reaching Dessie, the insurgents stumbled into the garrison of the 8th Airborne Brigade and the (North Korean-trained) 2nd Special Commando Brigade at Kutaber, where they were held up for three days. Outflanking this position, the EPRDF then overran several minor garrisons protecting the road between Woldya and Dessie instead. In this fashion, they forced the defenders of Kutaber and then Woldya to withdraw without a fight, and despite a latent lack of transportation.[45] Changing direction again, on 13 October 1989 the EPRDF overcame the garrison of Maranna (despite a diversionary counter-attack by the 5th Airborne Brigade), inflicting 1,521 casualties upon the government forces in the process.

To the great luck of the TRA, the insurgents ran themselves out of steam: although outmanoeuvred and repeatedly defeated, and having most of its divisions down to about 1,500 combatants each (a quarter of their nominal strength), the Ethiopian Army thus finally managed to stabilise its frontline by maintaining control over Dessie and Kimir Dengay. This hold was of a rather questionable nature: a mutiny erupted in Dessie when all the high-ranking officers and civilian officials left the town, the soldiers demanding their return. The panic spread all the way to Addis Ababa, where over 50,000 youngsters were drafted in November and December 1989 – often with brute force, and frequently through random kidnapping on the streets – and sent to training camps. Due to urgency, their training was reduced to one month, virtually guaranteeing that replacements sent to the battlefields were as poorly motivated as trained. The Derg was meanwhile so short on troops, that it mobilised even troops that had been captured by the TPLF and released after months of political re-education: once considered traitors because they had let themselves be taken captive, the former prisoners of war were submitted to another round of – this time governmental – political education, and then enlisted to form the 30th and 31st Infantry Divisions.[46]

Many of the TPLF's (and EPLA's) unit commanders involved in Operation Peace Through Struggle were very young: the commander of the 69th Battalion, visible on this still from a video, was a mere 30 years old. (Adrien Fontanellaz Collection)

Operation Maket

Alarming for the Derg as they were, the setbacks in Gonder prompted the MOND to reinforce the TRA massively, and then order it into a new offensive. The main aim of the resulting Operation Maket ('Defend') was to hit the EPRDF troop concentration in the mountains between Dessie and Debre Birhan with its new formation, Task Force 3B, consisting of the 3rd Infantry Division, the 102nd Airborne Division, the 3rd Paracommando Brigade, and the (North Korean-trained) Sparta Brigades designated 1/81/3, 2/81/1, and 2/81/3.[47] Furthermore, the 605th Corps was reinforced through the addition of the 15th and 95th Infantry Brigades, the 1/81/1 Sparta Brigade, and the 1033rd Commando Brigades, while the 603rd Corps' 7th Infantry Division (based in Kimir Dengay) was tasked with demonstrative attacks along the road from Woldya to Werata, with the aim of tying down enemy forces.

Operation Maket was launched on 19 December 1989, with the advance of Task Force 3B – spearheaded by the 3rd Infantry Division – along the dirt track linking Tebasit with Ali Doro. Despite fierce counterattacks, the Task Force slowly crept forward until taking Were Ilu, on 12 January 1990. However, rather than reacting to the Derg's initiative, the EPRDF opted to hit back in another place, and exercise pressure upon the 603rd and 605th Corps in the Kimir Dengay and Dessie areas, respectively. Hence, the battle was finally joined on three widely separated fronts.

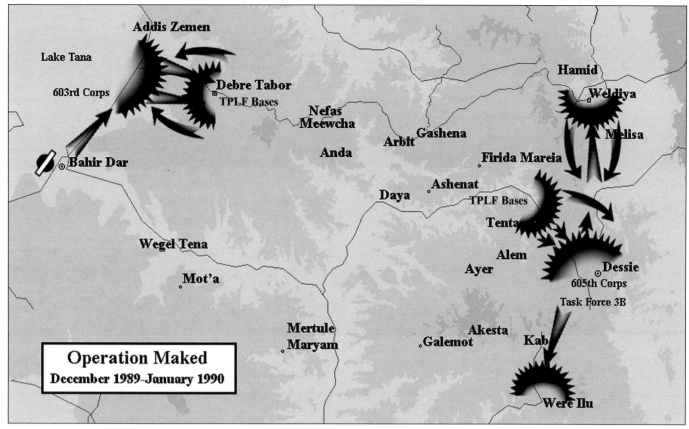

Map 4 Reconstruction of major manoeuvring during Operation Maket in December 1989. (Map by Tom Cooper)

The five brigades of the 603rd Corps – which advanced from Kimir Dengay on Nefas Meechwa – were stopped by the insurgent resistance. The EPRDF counterattack then regained all the ground lost, before continuing all the way to Kimir Dengay and Debre Tabor, which fell on 25 December 1989. With this, the Front was on the verge of severing the crucial road linking Bahir Dar with Gondar. Unsurprisingly, this triggered a massive reaction from the MOND: the 15th Infantry Division was detached from the SRA, and rushed to bolster defences of Bahir Dar and the Warrata crossroad, where it was joined by the 7th Infantry Division (which was on withdrawal from Debre Tabor), and the 25th Division. As soon as these three units were in position, the 603rd Corps counterattacked Debre Tabor, which it took on 6 January 1990, followed by Kimir Dengay, a few days later.

Operation Maket turned into a slugging match in the Dessie area too. On 21 December, the EPRDF overran the positions of the 115th Infantry Brigade in the Kuta Ber area. The 605th Corps reacted by counterattacking with three battalions drawn from the 15th Infantry and the 6th Mechanised Brigades, but was repulsed. A second, more powerful attempt was launched by the 86th and 504th Infantry Brigades. This proved more successful; however, the Ethiopians had lost Kuta Ber already the same evening. By 14 January 1990, the place was back under army control, when the EPRDF launched a nocturnal attack on positions of the 17th, 86th, 91st and 115th Infantry Brigades. The 91st Brigade was partially overrun, and it took a counterattack of the 5th Airborne Brigade and the 1/81/3 Sparta Brigade to recover the ground. However, this entire affair was only a deception plotted by the EPRDF – which meanwhile seized the town of Hayk, on the road linking Dessie with Woldya, and then repulsed the 1st Infantry Division's

counterattack. On 15 January, the 605th Corps counterattacked with the 2nd Paracommando, 6th Mechanised, 1033rd Commando, 17th, 16th, and 95th Infantry Brigades and retook Hayk. The insurgents secured the place in another counterattack, a day later, only to be forced out on 16 January 1990.

Despite this setback, the Front's strategy was proving successful because by this time the TRA felt forced to re-deploy the crack 3rd Infantry Division from Task Force 3B to the 605th Corps. Indeed, faithfully pursuing its tactics of delivering one blow in one sector, then changing the direction of its attacks, the EPRDF then attacked the 91st Infantry Brigade in Kuta Ber again, and overran even its headquarters. An Ethiopian counterattack forced it out of the area, three days later, but this was certainly no kind of contest that the Derg's military could sustain for any longer. Nevertheless, the MOND ordered the 605th Corps into the attack again. The 3rd and 8th Infantry Divisions pushed along the road from Dessie to Woldya, and took the towns of Wichale and Wurgesa, and then – between 27 January and 10 February 1990 – attempted to break through the Ninni Bar Pass towards Mersa. Rather easily, the EPRDF outflanked this advance and forced both units to withdraw towards Hayk.

Ultimately, although causing significant casualties, Operation Maket failed to break the insurgent concentration. It was foremost the spreading dissent within the EPRDF that brought an end to the fighting in this period: many of the Tigrayans who had joined the movement specifically to liberate Tigray, were not keen to fight in other provinces. Therefore, the TPLF's leadership was forced to impose a temporary stop, and launch a long and patient persuasion campaign to re-establish order and discipline in the movement.[48]

CHAPTER 4
THE END OF THE WAR IN ERITREA

Contrary to the TPLF, the EPLA restrained from launching large-scale operations in 1989. One of the reasons was significant losses that it had suffered during the highly successful Afabet campaign, which eventually forced the movement to introduce compulsory military service for all males and females in the areas it controlled. Because the EPLA was recruiting females too – and often forcefully – this measure found little sympathy in the Muslim parts of the population, and caused near-mutinies of the local population. The EPLF experienced quite significant problems along with accepting the fact that the population began questioning its claims to power, and often reacted by deploying military force to break resistance to forceful recruitment – in turn causing thousands to flee from the areas under its control. In other cases, up to 60% of those forcefully recruited had defected. Eventually, this recruitment crisis reached such proportions, that in 1990 the EPLF was forced to issue a 'national call' to the Eritreans living in the diaspora, and to recall most of its cadre from abroad.[49]

The crisis in its rear areas resulted in the Eritrean insurgency limiting its activity on the frontlines to touring foreign journalists around former battlefields, while only running minor combat operations – like harassing Ethiopian positions in the Semhar area, in the plains between Nakfa Mountains and the Red Sea. In January 1989, it claimed the destruction of 37 MBTs in this area, but provided no evidence in support. Certainly enough, the EPLA had run regular patrols around Keren, Asmara, and set up ambushes on the road linking the latter with Massawa. However, no attacks like earlier times were undertaken.

Instead, the Eritreans entered an alliance with the Afar Liberation Front and the Oromo Liberation Front, and reinforced the latter with its own commando units in order to ease its attacks on the road connecting Asseb with central Ethiopia.[50] Otherwise, most of their existing units had spent the year 1989 undergoing training in combined arms warfare. Thanks to the capture of large number of tanks and other armoured vehicles at Afabet, the insurgency greatly expanded its heavy weapons units, before it started activating new divisions too. Furthermore, the EPLA grew its naval branch through the introduction into service of numerous speedboats – including several 12-metre long *Simonneau Naja*-class vessels of French origin, acquired via Saudi Arabia. These were deployed for commando-style attacks, usually undertaken under cover of numerous islets along the Red Sea coast of Eritrea to avoid detection by the Ethiopian Navy. By January 1990, the EPLA's naval service began interdicting merchants underway for the ports of Asseb and Massawa, too. On the 3rd of that month, Polish merchant *Boreslaw Krywowsty* was heavily damaged and forced to run aground about 40 nautical miles from Masawa. The crew of 30 was captured by the EPLF. The next day, another Polish vessel, the merchant *Asnyk*, was targeted by coastal gunfire. On 10 January 1990, the crews of three speedboats intercepted and boarded the Yugoslav merchant *Kosta Stamenkovic*, and let it go only on condition that it would not dock at Massawa. Finally, on 23 January, a Soviet tanker was attacked, followed by the Danish *Svea Atlantica* on 12 February 1990.[51]

With many of its officers deeply involved in plotting the coup against Mengistu, the SRA was as inactive as the EPLA for much of 1989 – even more so once its headquarters was ordered by the MOND to release the 3rd and 15th Infantry, and the 102nd Airborne Divisions in favour of the TRA. Remaining units were meanwhile re-positioned to protect Keren, while the defence of Massawa and the road linking that port with Asmara was assigned to the 606th Corps, led by Brigadier-General Tilahun Kifle. The other main units controlled by this Corps were the 3rd Mechanised Division, and the 6th Infantry Division. However, these had to defend a very wide front and were badly overstretched. Under such conditions, no major operations were undertaken by any of them.

The only branch of the Ethiopian military active in Eritrea of early 1990 thus became the Ethiopian Air Force. The drought of summer resulted in an increase of relief activities, and thus the Ethiopian airmen soon found northern Eritrea full of 'interesting targets'. A journalist travelling with one of the trains from Sudan reported her experience as follows:

'The first sign of the impending raid on our convoy came on the morning of 29 January, when two MiGs bombed the nearby town of Serrano, a depot for food supplies. It is now under such constant attack that most of its inhabitants live in underground shelters and shop in the market under cover of darkness. In the afternoon, the jets switched their attack to our 11 lorries. They could have spotted us by the tell-tale glint of a wing mirror through the camouflage netting and branches. The MiGs attacked with cluster- and phosphorous bombs, scattering us over the arid terrain…After a brief lull, we were bombed again. Villagers, many of whom had come to help the wounded, scattered as the earth was chewed up by cannon fire and bombs.'[52]

Three lorries were destroyed, four tons of food burned, one local herder killed, and a driver and a cook injured on that occasion. Additional trucks belonging to ERA were burned in January, and on two occasions in March 1990.

Such air raids were not confined to northern Eritrea. The Wollega province, in the west of the country, was meanwhile the scene of bitter fighting between the government and the Oromo Liberation Front (OLF). Indeed, in January 1990 the OLF launched its largest military campaign to date, and briefly captured the town of Asosa. The government responded in predictable style. According to OLF claims, mostly substantiated by independent sources, the EtAF then bombed Asosa, on 7, 8, and 10 January 1990; Bambasi, on 15 January; Mandi, on 23 January; Dalatti, on 26 January; Bambasi and Hopha, on 27 January; Hurungu, on 7 February; Arge, Buldugilin, and Asosa on 8 February, burning hundreds of homes, killing livestock and hundreds of civilians.[53]

Training of Eritrean insurgent on a captured SPG-9 recoilless gun in the Tesseney area in the late 1980s. (Adrien Fontanellaz Collection)

A 'technical' of the EPLA with troops in action against an unknown Ethiopian position in early 1990. (Adrien Fontanellaz Collection)

Mi-24As of the EtAF usually deployed their 12.7mm machine gun and unguided 57mm rockets in their countless attacks on convoys carrying food and other relief aid from Sudan to Eritrea and Tigray in early 1990. (Herve Dessallier via Albert Grandolini)

Operation Fenkil

It is perfectly possible that the barbaric air strikes on civilians significantly contributed to the EPLF's decision to prepare a decisive blow against the SRA in early 1990: after all, nearly all of the MiG-21s and MiG-23s involved were operated by the units of the 2nd Command at Asmara airport, but frequently operating from Massawa airport too. Correspondingly, the insurgents mobilised four of their 6,500-strong divisions, together with numerous mechanised, artillery, and commando detachments from the 74th Division and from the Commando Division, and concentrated all of these in the Afabet area (for an order of battle of the forces involved in following operations in Eritrea, see Tables 6 and 7).

At 0100 hrs of 8 February 1990, the EPLA launched Operation Fenkil (after the name of Emperor Yohannes IV's horse, but also meaning 'to root out'). The aim of this enterprise was to breach the 200-kilometre long Ethiopian defence line that extended from Keren, east towards Ras Kobal, about 40 kilometres north of Massawa, and was defended by the 6th Infantry Division, headquartered at the locality named Sheeb, about 90 kilometres north of the port. Instead of attacking along the entire frontline, the EPLA focused all of its attention at Sheeb: in the course of

only three hours, the HQ of the 6th Division was overrun and its deputy commander, Lieutenant-Colonel Afewerke Tecle, captured.

Once through the enemy fortifications, the EPLA embarked on manoeuvring warfare and continued Operation Fenkil in the form of a three-pronged offensive in direction of the road between Massawa and Asmara. Despite often fierce resistance, this was reached by 9 February, by when the Eritreans seized the high ground near Dog'ali, following an armoured battle in which the insurgents captured ten tanks of the 6th Division, and forced the Ethiopians to fall back towards Dengolo, Dogali, and Gursugum. The SRA reacted by deploying the 18th Mountain Infantry Division and the 16th Mechanised Infantry Brigade from Ghinda along the road to Massawa, but both were blocked by ambushes and thus failed to reach the 606th Corps. The EtAF did react with up to 50 fighter-bomber sorties, but these effected next to nothing. Theoretically, the air force could have proved itself far more useful through airlifting the 15th Infantry Division and two additional Sparta Brigades from Bahir Dar to Massawa, as ordered by the headquarters of the SRA. However, that deployment was pre-empted by the quick insurgent advance. By the evening of 9 February, EPLA secured Gathelay, Dengelo and Dogali, forcing the 606th Corps to withdraw into the defence perimeter around the port. With this, the Massawa air base was within the range of their artillery: meaning not only that all the operational combat aircraft and helicopters had to be evacuated from there, but no reinforcements could be deployed with help of transport aircraft any more. Similarly, a series of daring actions by the EPLA's naval branch de-facto isolated the sea connection to the garrison, although the insurgents lost at least two of their speedboats in the process.[54]

Table 6: EPLF Order of Battle, Operation Fenkil, February 1990

Units	Commanders	Notes
Overall commander	Haile Samuel 'China'	
52nd Division	Filipos Woldeyohanes	
70th Division	Tekle Kifle 'Manjus'	
85th Division	Umar Hassan 'Tewil'	
96th Division	Sebhatu Like 'Wedi Like'	

Table 7: 606th Corps Order of Battle, Massawa, February 1990

Unit	Commander	Notes
606th Corps	Brigadier-General Tilahun Kifle	HQ in Massawa
3rd Mechanised Division	Brigadier-General Ali Hay Abdullah	4th Armoured-, 27th Mechanised Brigades
6th Infantry Division	Brigadier-General Teshome Tessema	

Training of EPLA female recruits at one of the camps in the Naqfa area. (Photo by Dan Connell)

A gunner of the EPLA with a 130mm calibre M54 cannon, of Soviet origin, during Operation Fenkil. (Albert Grandolini Collection)

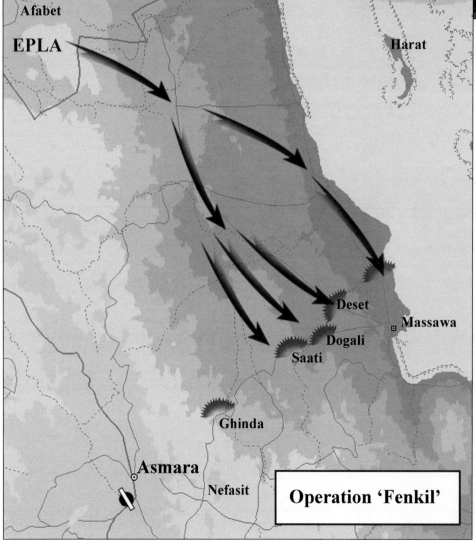

Map 5 Operation Fenkil, depicting the approximate approach routes taken by the EPLA. (Map by Tom Cooper)

Battle for Massawa

At dawn on 10 February 1990, the EPLA launched a general attack on the plain surrounding Massawa – in turn triggering the largest tank battle of the war, involving about 100 T-54s and T-55s from both sides. The first clash took place on the sandy coastal plain where, supported by T-55s and a fierce artillery barrage, the mechanised infantry of the EPLA clashed with Ethiopian armour. Two Ethiopian T-55s were knocked out in a matter of 15 minutes, causing panic among the entrenched defenders, who broke and ran. When the third tank was hit, the Eritreans charged over the sandy plains, racing ahead of their own armour in an attempt to catch the fleeing enemy. By the noon, the insurgents had reached the outskirts of the city.[55] Elsewhere, Eritrean armour systematically mauled the 4th Armoured and the 27th Mechanised Brigade, and during the ensuing pursuit the perimeter of the 606th Corps was split into two halves: one, commanded by Brigadier-Generals Kifle and Abdullah, withdrew into the naval base, at the bottom of a small peninsula, while the other – commanded by Brigadier-General Tessema – entrenched itself in Tualet ('Tewalot' for the Eritreans), connected with the mainland by a narrow causeway. By the evening of 10 February, the insurgents had invested the continental part of the city, finding themselves at the same positions as in late 1977. On the contrary, the Ethiopian garrison was in its death throws, cut off from the outside world.

During the night from 10 to 11 February 1990, the unfortunate defenders were finally reinforced by a company of Special Commandos, which arrived by ship from Asseb via the Dahlak archipelago. However, once on land, the defenders mistook the Ethiopian seamen for enemy infiltrators and went on a rampage, killing dozens in a close-quarters combat before realising their mistake. Furthermore, the ship that brought the Special Commandos to Massawa, and was to evacuate the wounded, was late in leaving, and then sunk by the EPLA's artillery. The latter plastered the naval base for the entire following day, sometimes with up to 200 shells a minute. The insurgents then deployed two captured T-55s – with their turrets turned towards their own lines to make defenders believe their own comrades were trying to rally them – to approach the Ethiopian lines. Turning their turrets around, both tanks then opened fire at close range, inflicting severe casualties before they were knocked out.

Late on 11 February, the EPLA issued two requests for the commander of the 6th Infantry Division to surrender Massawa or at least allow the civilian population to leave. However, either convinced that reinforcements were en route, or unaware of the actual position of his troops, Tessema refused. Instead, he gathered his troops at the end of the causeway in Tualot and awaited the inevitable. The EPLA decided to let him wait. On 12 February 1990, it launched an all-out assault on the naval base instead. Supported by murderous fire from all available heavy weapons, the insurgent infantry breached the perimeter and overwhelmed the defenders, capturing Brigadier-Generals Kifle and Abdullah in the process.

For the next two days, the EPLA continued pounding Tualot with all of its heavy weapons. In turn, the 2nd Command of the EtAF hit back in full force: however, instead of targeting the insurgent artillery, the first two MiG-23BNs that appeared on 16

February 1990, bombed the food warehouses and stockpiles of grain with CBUs filled with incendiaries. These burned about half of some 50,000 metric tons of US-donated wheat.[56] Additional air strikes continued hitting the city and the port: while these killed many civilians, they were of no help for the besieged Ethiopian troops, one of whom later recalled:

'The army sustained heavy casualties. The streets were filled with corpses and there was no one to bury them. A horrible stench pervaded the area. Many soldiers drowned themselves by jumping into the sea. There were corpses on the land, corpses in the sea. Most of the structures in the port and the houses in the city took fire from aerial bombardment. The area was polluted by the stench of the dead and the smoke from burning fuel.'

The relentless pounding of Tualot continued until 17 February, when the insurgents decided to assault. With no other solution on hand, they pushed their armour down the causeway. The Ethiopians hit the tanks with every weapon on hand, knocking out a number of them. However, the insurgents kept on coming, new T-55s replacing the tanks that were destroyed. At the height of the ensuing carnage, EPLA infantry embarked on fast boats assaulted the Tualot 'from behind'. Taken by surprise, the Ethiopians were slow to react to the emergence of the insurgent infantry and the latter managed to establish a small bridgehead. Now hit from two sides, the defenders fought back fiercely, but slowly began succumbing to the assault. Realising all was lost, Brigadier-General Tessema committed suicide, followed by about 150 other officers. Discouraged, the survivors gave up. That was the end of the 606th Corps.

The battle for Massawa cost the Ethiopians dearly. In addition to the disruption of their strategic supply lines, military losses included one mechanised and four infantry brigades. Around 8,000 officers and other ranks were captured, while 103 tanks, 62 other armoured vehicles, 157 artillery pieces, 137 anti-aircraft cannons, 76 mortars, 14 BM-21 MRLS and an ammunition dump with 37,544 shells were either destroyed or captured by the EPLA. Three MiG-21s and MiG-23s of the EtAF were shot down by ground fire, and all three pilots killed or captured.[57]

A still from a video showing a T-55 MBT of the 74th Division EPLA on advance in the direction of Massawa in February 1990. (Adrien Fontanellaz Collection)

Another vehicle in the same column was this M113 APC, captured from the Ethiopian Army and then overpained in sand colour. (Adrien Fontanellaz Collection)

An abandoned Ethiopian BMP-1 infantry fighting vehicle, with bodies of killed soldiers, on the streets of Massawa. (Adrien Fontanellaz Collection)

With the EPLA deploying all of its heavy arms, including most of the available tanks, the battle for Massawa saw one of biggest armoured clashes of the Ethiopian-Eritrean War of 1961-1991. This still from a video shows a line of T-54/55s from the 74th Division lined up along the coast opposite to the Tualot Peninsula. (Adrien Fontanellaz Collection)

This Ethiopian BTR-60 was knocked out during the fighting for the port of Massawa. (Adrien Fontanellaz Collection)

A T-54/55 of the 74th Division driving down the road inside Massawa. (Adrien Fontanellaz Collection)

EPLA troops watching two Ethiopian soldiers that defected from the Tualot Peninsula to reach their positions. (EPLF)

A trail of destruction: knocked out and abandoned BRDM-2 armoured scout cars of the Ethiopian Army along one of the roads leading into Massawa. (Adrien Fontanellaz Collection)

Major Getahun Demissie was one of the EtAF pilots known to have been shot down and killed over Eritrea. (EtAF via S. N.)

Revenge of the Ethiopian Air Force

Despite fierce fighting, the port of Massawa essentially remained intact. Unsurprisingly, the EtAF thus made the port a focus in the next phase of its counter-value campaign. Instead of striking the EPLA, and although the docks, commercial and residential quarters, and military bases in Massawa were well separated, and thus easy to distinguish from each other from the air, the Ethiopian Air Force concentrated all of its effort on hitting storage facilities and local civilians. For eight days after the fall of Massawa, these were subjected to repeated air strikes. The population quickly adapted to air raids and spent most of the day in shelters. Thus, relatively few civilians – about 25 – were killed, despite widespread deployment of Soviet and Israeli-made CBUs, often filled with incendiaries. The intensity of bombardment decreased by early March, until the EPLF announced that the port was ready for re-opening, and appealed for relief shipments of food. As soon as the first merchant set sail for Massawa – the Danish-flagged ship *Danika 4* – the Derg ordered the EtAF into a series of sustained air strikes. In four air raids on 4 and 5 April 1990, at least 71 people were killed and hundreds injured by general purpose bombs, which caused severe damage to warehouses and diverse installations in the port, and destroyed more than 100 homes. Furthermore, over 70 civilians were killed and nearly 200 injured in air strikes that hit Afabet and Koro on the same days. Another particularly devastating air strike hit Massawa again on 8 April:

> 'ERA officials familiar with the government military tactics are shocked by a new kind of bomb which has only been used since the Massawa takeover. Everyone in the town is talking about this new kind of bomb, which destroys everything with a 100 metre radius, and which is particularly effective in the shanty areas with flimsy housing structures. These cluster bombs were almost certainly supplied by the Israeli government.'[58]

At 1030 hrs in the late morning of 22 April 1990, Massawa was bombed by two MiG-23BNs which deployed parachute-retarded bombs this time. Other than material damage, no casualties occurred because most of the population took refuge inside bomb shelters. However, another pair of MiG-23BNs appeared at low altitude at dusk, around 1815 hrs, taking everybody by surprise. This time, the pilots dropped at least two CBUs directly over a crowded street in the centre of the town: over 50 civilians were killed instantly, while more than 50 succumbed to their injuries in the following hours and days.[59]

A few days later, as the next chartered freighter carrying relief aid was approaching Massawa, Addis Ababa threatened to bomb the ship should it attempt to dock – and refused to relent despite intensive diplomatic pressure. The Derg gave up only on 10 June 1990 – and then in the face of intensive pressure from Washington. By then, the port facilities had been virtually destroyed by air strikes.

A column of EPLA technicals – mounting 37mm anti-aircraft cannons – moving down a street inside Massawa in 1990. (Adrien Fontanellaz Collection)

In reaction to Ethiopian air strikes, the EPLA deployed a large number of anti-aircraft artillery pieces around its most important bases – and also in Massawa. While these had shot down several Ethiopian fighter-bombers over time, their effectiveness remained limited in overall scope. (Albert Grandolini Collection)

Pilots from one of the EtAF's MiG-23BN squadrons, as seen in the late 1980s. They flew most of the highly destructive air strikes on Massawa in April 1990. (EtAF via S.N.)

Siege of Asmara

Although the EPLA suffered far heavier losses in the course of the battle for Massawa than it was ever ready to admit, it was also reinforced to unprecedented levels by the loot from depots of the 606th Corps. On the contrary, the loss of the vital port meant the virtual death sentence of the SRA: as of March 1990, its troops garrisoning Asmara and Keren were left with only one intact link to Addis Ababa – the airport of Asmara. Correspondingly, the EtAF intensified its air bridge to the Eritrean capital, its transports flying up to 20 sorties a day, instead of the usual 4 to 6. However, even this effort was anything but sufficient: because the Ethiopian military prevented the locals from leaving Asmara, it was forced to feed them. Unsurprisingly, by June 1990, the SRA's depots in the Asmara area were down to food-reserves worth only 10 days.[60]

Meanwhile, the EPLA moved out to tighten the noose about the Eritrean capital. In March 1990, it launched a series of attacks on the SRA's defensive lines east and north of Asmara. Although most of these were repulsed, the insurgents eventually managed to reach the Ala and Bizen areas, about 25 kilometres from the city, from where its artillery was within range of the airport. The following campaign of shelling had closed the airport on numerous occasions. On 1 March 1990, an aircraft carrying relief aid was hit while unloading, and one civilian was killed. A Boeing 707 of the Ethiopian Airlines aircraft carrying fuel was hit by a shell and burned out, on 22 March 1991, while on 26 April another airliner was damaged and three passengers killed. In addition to civilian aircraft, shelling damaged a number of EtAF machines, including at least two MiGs, and the local ammunition dump. As well as the airport, the insurgent shelling hit multiple residential areas, destroying over 100 homes and killing more than 60 civilians between March and June 1990. Such attacks prompted many people to try to flee. Those who could had bribed the authorities to get a place on one of airliners and transport aircraft; however, the mass of the people couldn't. Whoever was caught while attempting to flee on land was subjected to summary arrest and detention.[61]

The populations of Asmara and Keren were not only terrorised by the siege and behaviour of Ethiopian military and security services: they also feared the insurgents might repeat the massacre that had accompanied their attack on the Eritrean capital in January 1975.[62] In turn, the fear of similar losses to those at Massawa, and of air strikes deterred the EPLA from launching an all-out attack on Asmara – at least until the EtAF lost its bases in Bahir Dar and Debre Zeit, nearly a year later. Instead, the Eritrean insurgents limited their activity to grinding down the defensive perimeters around Asmara, Keren, Decamere, Mendefere and Adi Keyh. Their only bigger operation was the capture of Senafe in May 1990.

Although critically short on food, the SRA was far from being beaten. This became obvious in August 1990, when a large attack by the EPLA on Decamere was easily repulsed by the 609th Corps. In September, the second attempt experienced the same fate. Indeed, after the end of the rainy season, in October 1990, the EtAF returned to the skies over Eritrea and hit not only civilians, but also all the recognized insurgent positions causing heavy losses to their artillery and tank units. Emboldened, in mid-October 1990, the SRA launched several attacks in the Asmara and Decamere areas, regaining control over several crucial positions. Although the insurgents then counterattacked and reached a point 18 kilometres from Asmara airport, overall the situation in Eritrea as of late 1990 was that of a stalemate: the SRA held firmly onto Asmara, Keren, Mendefera, Chinda, and Decamere. Strategists of the EPLA were thus forced to wait for a better opportunity.[63]

A D-30 122mm howitzer of the EPLA in action against Asmara Airport in early 1990. (Adrien Fontanellaz Collection)

A ruined home in Decamere, as seen after the end of the war. (Photo by Dan Connell)

In the mid-1990s, the surviving Mi-8s of the EtAF were overhauled by the DAVEC. Ever since, the entire fleet has worn this disruptive camouflage pattern (which is applied in exactly the same form on all of the helicopters in question), consisting of dark beige and dark green on upper surfaces and sides, and light blue on the undersides. Although not visible on any of the photographs taken immediately afterwards, sand filters installed on air intakes are still regularly used in operations. Ethiopian Mi-8s are almost exclusively deployed for transport and liaison purposes and thus next to never armed. Their serials – always applied in yellow – remain in the same dimensions and range as applied at earlier times. (Artwork by Tom Cooper)

The true workhorse of the EtAF during the Badme War was its fleet of Mi-24A helicopter gunships. They flew hundreds, if not thousands of CAS sorties, keeping Eritrean frontlines under constant pressure throughout two years of the war. By the time of this conflict, all had been overhauled at DAVEC, where they received a new camouflage pattern – similar to that of Ethiopian Mi-35s – consisting of beige (BS381C/388) and dark green (with a strong bluish touch), and light admiralty grey (BS381C/697) on undersurfaces. Their usual armament consisted of two or four UB-32-57 pods for S-5 57mm unguided rockets, and their internal 12.7mm machine-gun. This helicopter is shown with the national marking of the 'Federal Democratic Republic of Ethiopia', introduced in December 1998. Serials known as operational in the 1998-2001 period were 1616, 1621, 1622, 1624, and 1627. (Artwork by Tom Cooper)

Although meanwhile overhauled at DAVEC, Ethiopian Mi-35s were still wearing the same camouflage pattern as applied in the former USSR, prior to delivery. This consisted of beige (BS381C/388) and dark green on top surfaces and sides, and light admiralty grey (BS381C/697) on undersurfaces. Contrary to Mi-24As, the background for the warning insignia 'Danger' on their rear fuselage is painted in red. All the helicopter gunships of this type were still regularly equipped with chaff and flare dispensers installed under the rear part of the boom. While the fleet was compatible with guided anti-tank missiles, these were never carried – principally as a weight-saving measure. Serials known as operational in 1998-2001 period were 2101, 2105, 2107, 2108 (captured intact by Eritreans), and 2110 (shown here). (Artwork by Tom Cooper)

The Ethiopian Air Force acquired no less than 80 MiG-21bis fighter-bombers in the period 1977-1984, and they wore serials from 1051 to 1130. All were camouflaged in diverse variants of the same camouflage pattern, consisting of beige (BS381C/388) and dark olive drab (BS381C/298) on top surfaces and sides, and light admiralty grey (BS381C/697) on undersurfaces. By 1989, they were the principal armament of up to eight different squadrons. This example – one of the last four delivered to Ethiopia, and last seen at Debre Zeit AB in the mid-2000s – is illustrated with two types of the most frequently used bombs: FAB-250M-62 on the inboard underwing pylon, and a RBK-250PTAB on the outboard pylon, although the usual armament consisted of only two bombs of 250 or 500kg. (Artwork by Tom Cooper)

With their attrition remaining relatively limited during the 1980s, the EtAF was still in possession of a large number (about 60) of MiG-21bis airframes when it was re-established in the period 1992-1995. About 20 of these were overhauled and returned to service by the time of the Badme War. Although meanwhile overhauled by the DAVEC, and receiving chaff and flare dispensers low on the rear fuselage, all retained their original camouflage pattern in beige and olive drab, although this was applied in very diverse fashions. Early during the new war with Eritrea, they formed the backbone of the Ethiopian interceptor fleet, and flew hundreds of combat air patrols armed with venerable R-13M and R-60MK air-to-air missiles, as illustrated here. In December 1998, all the survivors received the new national insignia, and had their serial re-positioned slightly forward on the fin. (Artwork by Tom Cooper)

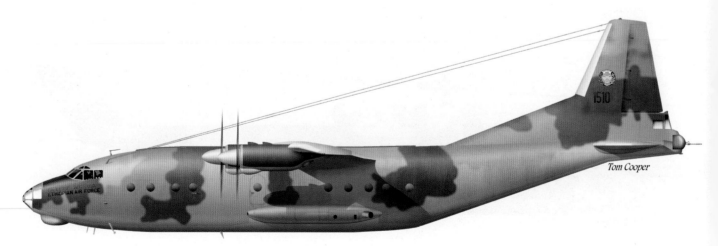

The EtAF's fleet of An-12 transports was down to five or six aircraft by 1998. However, as indispensable assets, they were meanwhile all overhauled and returned to service – now wearing an attractive camouflage pattern consisting of tan and olive drab or dark green (usually applied atop their original grey overall colours). From December 1998, new national insignia was applied in place on the fin where Ethiopian An-12s used to wear their serial numbers, with serials directly below it. (Artwork by Tom Cooper)

Fewer than half of the 44 MiG-23BNs acquired by Ethiopia in the period 1978-1985 remained intact by 1991, but they remained the backbone of the EtAF's fighter-bomber fleet. Starting in the late 1980s, some of the aircraft in question were overhauled at DAVEC, and received a new camouflage pattern, consisting of tan, dark brown and dark green. The latter two colours tended to get bleached by the sun quite quickly, early on, but their quality improved significantly ever since. Principal armament of Ethiopian MiG-23BNs in the late 1980s and early 1990s consisted of CBUs, including (see insets) Soviet-made RBK-250PTAB and RBK-500s, and Israeli-made TAL-1/2/3s. Due to constraints imposed by the local geography and climate, the usual warload consisted of only two bombs of up to 500kg: heavier loads were carried only for 'special' missions. (Artwork by Tom Cooper)

By the time the Badme War erupted in 1998, all of the remaining Ethiopian MiG-23BNs were overhauled by the DAVEC and received diverse variants of the camouflage pattern depicted here. This still consisted of tan, dark brown and dark green (with a strong bluish touch). Serials of aircraft known to have been operational as of 1998-2001 were 1251, 1257, 1265, 1266, 1269, 1270, 1276, 1285, 1288, 1289, 1290, 1296 and 1297. Other than RBK-250PTABs, their primary armament consisted of FAB-500M-62 bombs (illustrated here), UB-32-57 pods for 57mm unguided rockets and also S-24 heavy 240mm unguided rockets. (Artwork by Tom Cooper)

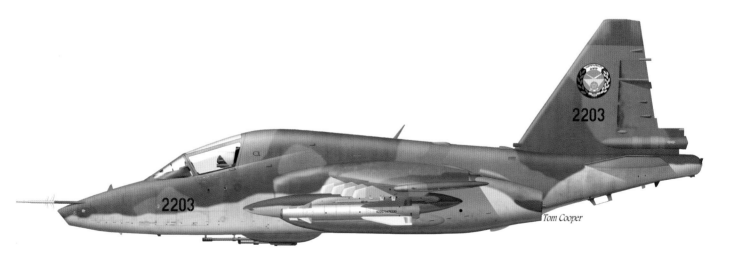

Very little is known about the four Su-25s delivered to Ethiopia in late 1999, except that they were all second-hand aircraft from the stocks of the Russian air force. The first two were Su-25UB, two-seat conversion trainers, apparently wearing serials 2201 and 2202. The other two – apparently wearing serials 2203 and 2204 – were Su-25Ts: this was a reasonably advanced variant, compatible with precision guided ammunition – including Kh-29 (AS-14 Kedge) guided bombs, one of which is illustrated here. All four aircraft retained their camouflage patterns applied before delivery. In the case of this one, this consisted of dark brown (FS30372), dark green (FS34088), and grey-green (FS34424) or green (FS34102) on top surfaces and sides, and light admiralty grey on undersurfaces. (Artwork by Tom Cooper)

All of the Su-27s acquired by Ethiopia were early-built, second hand aircraft from the stocks of the Russian Air Force. While designated Su-27SKs, they had had some of their equipment (foremost their IFF-systems) replaced, and were armed with downgraded R-27ER/ET air-to-air missiles (shown in inset), but were otherwise the same as Russian-flown aircraft. Correspondingly, their camouflage pattern originally consisted of light blue (FS25550) overall, with a camouflage pattern of blue (FS25440) on top surfaces. It is possible that some had originally had some light grey (FS36480) applied on diverse parts of the airframe. All the dielectric panels were painted in cream white (FS17925), though some had their fin-tips painted in green (FS14110) too. The Su-27SK shown here, serial 1954, was claimed to have scored the first kill for this type in Ethiopia – against an Eritrean MiG-29 – on 25 February 1999. (Artwork by Tom Cooper)

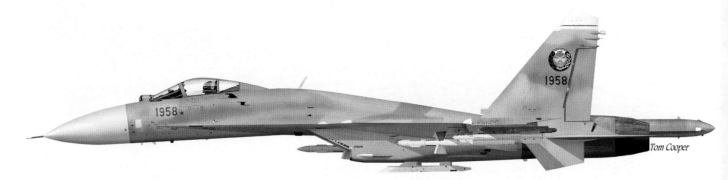

The second aerial victory against Eritrean MiG-29s, scored on 26 February 1999, was achieved by Lieutenant-Colonel Gebre Haile-Selassie, while flying this Su-27SK, serial number 1958. The aircraft wore the same camouflage pattern in light blue (overall) and blue, perhaps some light grey too. In commemoration of Haile-Selassie's victory, a 'kill marking' – in the form of a red star – was applied on either side of the cockpit, directly behind the serial number. The aircraft is illustrated in one of two standard warloads deployed during that conflict: with a pair of R-27ERs between intakes, one R-27ET on each of the two centre underwing pylons, and one R-73E on each of outboard underwing pylons. Wing-tip pylons were usually left empty. (Artwork by Tom Cooper)

Although frequently flown by combined, Ethiopian-Russian crews, and thus staying away from the combat zone, Su-27UBKs of No. 6 Squadron, EtAF, are said to have played a very important role in all intercepts of Eritrean MiG-29s. They wore the same camouflage pattern as that applied on single-seaters but – due to their intensive use for conversion training of Ethiopian pilots – this was usually worn out beyond recognition. Furthermore, their serials, applied on the forward fuselage, were positioned lower than those applied on single-seat Su-27SKs. Their warloads were the same as those of single-seaters, consisting of a pair each of R-27ERs, R-27ETs and R-73Es. Notable is that, because they were delivered only after the EtAF had introduced its new national insignia, Ethiopian Su-27s never wore the national markings consisting of a green roundel with red inside field and a yellow star. Furthermore, and as far as can be assessed from available photographs, they never received any national insignia on top or undersurfaces of their wing. (Artwork by Tom Cooper)

The Eritrean Air Force acquired at least four ex-EtAF Mi-8s and a similar number of Mi-17s during the mid-1990s. All were operated by No. 8 Squadron, ERAF, and painted in a camouflage pattern similar to this one, including light tan and red brown on top surfaces and sides, and light blue-grey on undersurfaces. All were armed, too: usually with UB-32-57 pods for 57mm unguided rockets, but at least as often with 9-A-624 pods for 23mm cannons. (Artwork by Tom Cooper)

The four MB.339s acquired by Ethiopia were all painted in the same camouflage pattern, consisting of light yellow sand and dark green on top surfaces and sides, and light blue on undersurfaces (sadly, exact shades remain unknown). Operated by No. 4 Squadron, ERAF, the Macchis were originally used for basic and advanced jet training. However, equipped with a very advanced nav/attack platform, they saw a lot of action early during the Badme War, usually armed with two CBUs. The exact type acquired by Ethiopia remains unknown, but illustrated is the 'most likely candidate': a Spanish-made BME-330C. Furthermore, they frequently carried gun-pods containing a 30mm DEFA 553 cannon with 120 rounds (one such pod was carried under each wing). (Artwork by Tom Cooper)

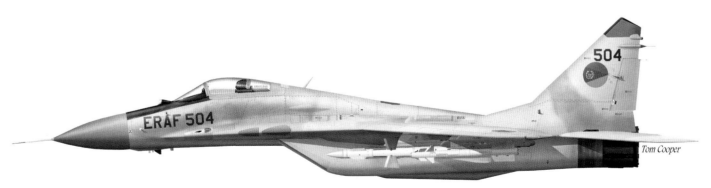

The most advanced type in service with the ERAF as of 1998-1999 were five MiG-29s (9.12s) and one MiG-29UB (9.51) – the deliveries of which prompted the Ethiopians into a hurried acquisition of Su-27s. Overhauled before delivery, Eritrean MiG-29s originally wore the standard camouflage pattern consisting of light grey (FS26373) overall, with wide strips of grey-green (FS35352) on the upper surfaces. This suffered heavily under the local climate and was usually unrecognizable after the first year of their service with Eritrea. National markings were applied in four positions: on outer sides of each fin, top surface of the left and bottom surface of the right wing. Serials were always prefixed by the title 'ERAF', as illustrated here. Their primary armament consisted of two R-27R/Ts, carried on inboard underwing stations, and a pair of R-73Es, always installed on outboard underwing pylons only. (Artwork by Tom Cooper)

The most powerful tank in service in Ethiopia from the mid-1980s, though to the 1990s, and well into the 2000s, was the T-62M. About 100 of these were acquired of which some 74-75 remained operational by the time of the Badme War. While photographs of them remain rare, as far as can be assessed, they never received any kind of specific markings or other insignia. (Artwork by David Bocquelet)

T-54s and T-55s captured by the EPLA from the Ethiopian Army in the 1980s were usually left in their original livery (dark olive green). While some received insignia in the form of turret numbers (applied in white), no details about these are known. What is certain is that all the T-54/55s of the 74th Division EPLA deployed for the assault of Massawa wore vertical stripes in yellow on their turret sides. Some had their rear fuel tanks painted in yellow or brick-red, too. (Artwork by David Bocquelet)

By the time of the Badme War, the Ethiopian Army was in the process of overhauling a large number of its surviving T-54/55s. Most of them were sent to the frontlines wearing diverse versions of the camouflage pattern illustrated here, consisting of their original colour (dark olive green), with stripes of black and yellow or sand applied in a wavy pattern. To make their identification easier, their crews often added an Ethiopian flag somewhere on the cannon tube. (Artwork by David Bocquelet)

Ethiopia acquired a relatively small number – perhaps 60 in total – of BMP-1s in the late 1980s. They originally served with the SDB, based in Addis Ababa, but a few were present in Masswa, when that port was attacked by the EPLA in February 1990. As far as can be assessed from available photos, all were originally left in dark olive drab overall. By 1998, most of about 20 survivors were overhauled and received a disruptive pattern in different shades of green, as illustrated here. (Artwork by David Bocquelet)

Amongst the more exotic vehicles in ENDF's arsenal during the Badme War were M1977 self-propelled howitzers made in North Korea. Essentially being a D-30 howitzer of Soviet design installed on the chassis of the YW-531 armoured personnel carrier, it is roughly equivalent in overall capability to the Soviet/Russian-made 2S1 Gvozdika. As far as is known, all the Ethiopian examples retained their original green overall colour. (Artwork by David Bocquelet)

Ethiopia acquired about a dozen modern 2S19 Msta-S self-propelled 152mm howitzers from Russia in late 1998. All arrived still wearing their original camouflage pattern of dark olive drab overall, and some received turret numbers as illustrated here. This artillery piece outranged everything in the Eritrean arsenal, thus greatly increasing the ENDF's superiority in firepower vis-à-vis the ERDF. (Artwork by David Bocquelet)

By 1999, some Ethiopian T-54/55s received an upgrade similar to the T-55AM or T-55AM1 kit, including add-on armour on hull and turret-fronts, and rubber side skirts. Such tanks were sighted for the first time during Operation Sunset in February 1999. Their camouflage pattern was similar to that of numerous T-54/55s overhauled at an earlier time, and consisted of stripes in dark green or black and yellow sand colours. (Artwork by David Bocquelet)

By 1998, most ERDF-operated T-54/55s were overpainted in diverse shades of yellow or sand colours – all of which were quite quickly bleached by the sun and sand. The yellow dot remained the typical – and usually the only – identification insignia of Eritrean-operated tanks. (Artwork by David Bocquelet)

The ERDF acquired a batch of about a dozen 2S1 Gvozdika self-propelled howitzers by 1998, and these saw intensive service early during the Badme War. As far as is known about them, all received diverse disruptive camouflage patterns, usually consisting of sand or light green and brown colours, applied on their original coat of dark olive brown. (Artwork by David Bocquelet)

Operation Dankalia

The opportunity sought for by the Eritreans opened only in February 1991, by when the Derg was in its death throws. Scrambling to mobilise all available units, the EPLA then launched Operation Dankalia on 21 February – and then in an unexpected direction: its 491 Corps, which included the 16th and 70th Divisions, reinforced by tanks and artillery, advanced over the desert plains along the Red Sea to the port of Asseb. Although venturing into an area where the population was not particularly supportive of the insurgency, this move was expected to finish off the Derg, because that port was still connected to Addis Ababa by a good-quality paved road, and contained the only oil refinery in all of Ethiopia. Even then, Operation Dankalia became possible only because the Ethiopian Navy essentially melted away following the loss of Massawa. Furthermore, the Soviets were in the process of evacuating their base in the Dahlak archipelago. Thus, the EPLA was free to not only use its naval branch to move supplies, but also advance undisturbed along the coast.

Striking into a virtual vacuum, the 491 Corps advanced quickly and, on 27 February 1991, attacked the town of Tiyo, defended only by the 141th Infantry Brigade (5th Infantry Division). Coordinating their assault with that of their naval branch, the insurgents secured the place on 1 March, mauling the Ethiopian brigade in the process. The advance was then continued in direction of the village of Idd, secured on 8 March following a battle in which the EPLA claimed the destruction of five – and the capture of four – Ethiopian tanks. Several days later, the Eritreans reached Beylul, the last town north of Asseb.

Recognizing the threat, the Ethiopian Army reacted by deploying reinforcements to the vital port, despite the generally critical situation all over the country. Correspondingly, the EtAF deployed a full squadron of MiG-21bis and MiG-23BN fighter-bombers each, while the Army Aviation Battalion added a company of Mi-35 helicopters to Asseb airport – located roughly halfway between the port and Beylul. The aircraft and helicopters went into action on 18 March, when they hit multiple insurgent columns in the open, causing heavy casualties. The EPLA reacted by outflanking the garrison of Beylul and striking straight for

While fighting the advance of Eritrean insurgents on Asseb, the EtAF deployed even its vaunted MiG-23ML interceptors as fighter-bombers. For this purpose, several mounts from its No. 10 Squadron was forward-deployed at Asseb airport: one was eventually abandoned there. (EtAF via S.N.)

Assab, launching a mad race to reach the airport only a day later. Repeatedly hit by air strikes, its advance then collided frontally with the well-entrenched 5th Infantry Division, meanwhile reinforced by two tank battalions. Furthermore, EtAF fighter-bombers destroyed the EPLA's logistic base in Tiyo, on 30 March, and sunk several supply vessels. Concluding they had no chance of taking Asseb, the Eritreans turned on Beylul and captured it, following two days of bitter battle with the defending 17th Infantry Brigade, on 6 April 1991.

Sudden End

In May 1991, EPLF ordered the main concentration of EPLA forces into the definitive blow against the Asmara pocket. Mid-morning on 19 May 1991, a fierce artillery barrage announced the insurgents' assault on Decamere. The SRA promptly reacted by deploying reinforcements from the 10th Infantry and 18th Mountain Infantry Divisions, and the 29th Mechanised Brigade, plus two Sparta Brigades. These helped retain the town, but failed to prevent the insurgents from taking the critical Mounta Arar, near Gura. After regrouping, the EPLA was thus able to take Decamere in the course of a pitched street battle on 23 May 1991: this was one of fiercest of the entire war, and when it ended, several insurgent battalions were down to a mere 10% of their nominal strength. Indeed, the commander of the 81st Brigade EPLA (61st Division), subsequently recalled:

'...this is not a battlefield. It is hell. No living creature is expected to survive it.'

With its situation becoming hopeless, the headquarters of the SRA in Asmara announced the capitulation of the Ethiopian military in Eritrea on the following day. While the garrisons of Ghinda, Mendefera, and Adi Kwala followed the corresponding

EPLA insurgents advancing down the coastal road in a southern direction during Operation Dankalia in February 1991. (EPLF)

order, dozens of thousands of soldiers and members of the civilian administration from Asmara and Keren, together with their families, decided to escape to Sudan. Forming a giant column including hundreds of trucks and several dozens of armoured vehicles, they broke through along the road to Agordat. Although thousands of them died underway – few in combat, many of thirst – at least 14,000 managed to reach Sudan. Similarly, the garrison of Asseb refused to capitulate and withdrew into Djibouti instead. The last few remaining units of the Ethiopian Navy either followed in fashion, or sailed all the way to Saudi Arabia and Yemen – leaving the EPLA to take the port on 26 May 1991. When all the Ethiopian resistance in Eritrea ceased, the EPLA thus captured only about 82,000 Ethiopian military personnel, and about 44,000 dependants.[64]

Long after the end of the war, mines continued endangering the lives of the Ethiopian and Eritrean population. Most had to be removed by rather simple means – usually by hand. (Photo by Dan Connell)

CHAPTER 5
DOWNFALL OF THE DERG

Although the EPLF/EPLA did not distinguish themselves with any further large-scale operations after capturing Massawa, their cooperation with the EPRDF paid handsome dividends. The fall of Massawa not only destroyed the 606th Corps of the Ethiopian Army, but significantly weakened the 603rd Corps, which was forced to re-assign its 15th Infantry Division to the SRA. This happened around the same time the EPRDF was in the process of preparing a new offensive, involving not only the battle-hardened Aurora, Agazi and May Day Divisions, but also the recently established Maqdala and Maebal Division. Furthermore, the EPLA had deployed up to three brigades to Ethiopia, in support of the EPRDF. Two of these were mechanised units: one deployed in Gondar, and the other in Wollo.[65]

Although the Ethiopian military intelligence detected the concentration of these forces in the Kimir Dengay area, opposite to the 603rd Corps, on time, the TRA was not in a position to take any kind of meaningful pre-emptive action. The 603rd Corps was down to only the 7th and 25th Infantry Divisions and the 102nd Airborne Division, all of which were exhausted and depleted. True enough, these units were reinforced through the addition of up to 9,500 new troops, but at least 4,500 of these were hastily trained recruits, while the rest were former prisoners of war released by the insurgents. Finally, most of these troops were assigned to the 25th and the 102nd Divisions, while the 7th Infantry remained badly understrength: each of its brigades had only around 800 troops.

Collapse in Kimir Dengay

Such details did not escape the attention of the EPRDF's reconnaissance, which found numerous gaps between major Ethiopian positions. Correspondingly, when they initiated their attack, on the evening of 25 February 1990, the Maqdala and Maebal Divisions frontally assaulted the forward lines of the 2nd, 28th and 133rd Infantry and the 25th Motorised Brigades. This offered an opportunity for the Alula Division to infiltrate

the same Ethiopian units and then collapse them by destroying their rear positions. Similarly, the Aurora Division – supported by the diversionary frontal attack of the Agazi Division that tied down the 33rd and the 155th Infantry Brigades – pushed through a gap separating the 33rd from the 155th Infantry Brigade, and then turned around to attack the former, and the 5th Airborne Brigade, in the back. Although receiving the timely order to do so, the 155th Infantry Brigade failed to counterattack the exposed flank of the Aurora Division. The final coup was delivered by the May Day Division, which made a wide flanking movement before advancing on the Alem Saga Pass on the road linking Debre Tabor with Werata.

In a matter of only two days, the 603rd Corps fell apart – foremost because its chain of command collapsed when several headquarters were overrun, while many units succumbed to multi-prong attacks of numerically superior and far more manoeuvrable forces. Some of its units – like the 7th Airborne Brigade and the 25th Infantry Division – fought fiercely and held their positions, repulsing numerous assaults. The mauled 7th Infantry Division was the first to fall back: the 25th Infantry Division held out until the death of its commander, Colonel Mulgeta Mammo. However, nothing the Ethiopians experienced by that point in time was comparable to what happened on 26 February, when the main ammunition dump in Debre Tabor received a direct hit from assaulting EPRDF troops. The resulting detonation panicked thousands of the Ethiopian troops and caused them to flee en masse towards Werata. Unable to regain control, the commander of the 603rd Corps, Brigadier-General Abbaba Haile Sellase had no choice but to follow the mob. Debre Tabor thus fell into insurgent hands on 27 February 1990.

Worse was to follow, the Ethiopians not only had to punch through the blocking position of the May Day Division on the Alem Saga Pass: determined not to let the enemy sort out the chaos, the EPRDF followed in hot pursuit. Its first few shells fired on Werata triggered another mass panic, causing an outright stampede of thousands of troops all the way to Bahir Dar. The chaos reached such proportions, that the flight was barely slowed down by officers that blew up the bridge across the Blue Nile. Altogether, in only six days of fighting the EPRDF had destroyed three Ethiopian divisions, and reached the positions within striking distance of Bahir Dar – major base of the 4th Command, EtAF.[66]

Amongst the insurgent units deployed for the next major operation against the Ethiopian military in early 1990 were at least three brigades of the EPLA. This still from a video shows one of the technicals operated by Eritrean insurgents – and mounting a ZU-23 AA cannon – in action. (Adrien Fontanellaz Collection)

EPLA combatants waiting for signal to resume their advance. (Albert Grandolini Collection)

Operation Flame

Having secured the Werata, and in expectation of the usual Ethiopian counterattack, the insurgents spent the next few weeks entrenching themselves in the mountains surrounding the plain between that town and Bahir Dar. When nothing of that kind happened, the leadership of the EPRDF decided to resume the offensive – this time through advancing into the triangle formed by the towns of Dessie, Debre Bihan and Debre Marqos. In this fashion, they expected not only to create a wedge between whatever was left of the 603rd and the 605th Corps, which had its main base in Dessie: indeed, from this area, they could isolate either of the two groups of forces from Addis Ababa, and then destroy them in detail.[67]

Initially at least, this operation proved highly successful: between 25 and 30 March 1990, the EPRDF dislodged the Ethiopians from their positions between Rema and Alem Katema, while by 8 April, the insurgents seized Rabel and Mahal Meda, too. On 12 April, their advance parties managed to temporarily cut off the road linking Dessie with Addis Ababa but were forced back by a powerful counterattack of the 1st Infantry Division after two days of bitter fighting. However, the MOND then began piling reinforcements in to the Dessie area by deploying not only a brigade-sized task force of the SDB, but also the 19th, 89th and 164th Infantry Brigades, the 6th Mechanised and the 1035th Commando Brigades, the 3/82/3, 4/82/1, 4/82/2, and 4/82/3 Sparta Brigades, and a full battalion of BM-24 MRLS there. Finally, it ordered most of these into a counterattack, and thus the 19th and 89th Infantry Brigades, the 6th Mechanised, and the 3/82/3 Sparta Brigades recaptured Mehal Meda on 19 April 1990.[68]

Emboldened by this – actually minor – success, the Ethiopian military then came to the idea of crushing the entire concentration of the EPRDF in northern Shewa Province. Correspondingly, it deployed the 1st, 3rd, and 4th Infantry Divisions, and the entire 102nd Airborne Division into a major offensive along multiple routes, seeking to find, encircle and destroy the enemy. In an attempt to prevent diversionary attacks like those on the Task Force 3B in the same area, in February 1990, it reinforced the 605th Corps in Dessie with the 26th and 27th Infantry Divisions, and the 3/82/3, 4/82/1, and 4/82/3 Sparta Brigades. Finally, the 6th Mechanised Brigade was deployed to Debra Sina as a reserve. The mission of these was not only to hold off any enemy counteroffensive, but also to block the EPRDF's main line of retreat.

The resulting Operation Nebelbal (Flame) was initiated on 21 May 1990, with the 102nd Airborne Division establishing itself between Lemi and the Jamma River, while the 1st Infantry Division secured the areas of Mehal Meda and Rabet. The 3rd Infantry advanced along the road from Dessie to Rema, and took Kabe, Were Ilu and Degolo in quick succession. The 8th Infantry Division came up next, securing the rear. What the Ethiopians did not know was that these early successes were all possible because the EPRDF decided to withdraw without fighting, and instead concentrate in the Alem Ketema area, where it could anchor its lines on such strongpoints as the old fortress of Karra Mesheg. From there, they were able to fight each of advancing Ethiopian units separately, before these could approach the insurgent defence lines and deliver a simultaneous attack.

Unaware of the trap in front of them, the Ethiopian Army continued advancing until 22 May, when the EPRDF ambushed the 102nd Airborne Division on the Jamma River: while the main insurgent force delivered a frontal assault on the 5th and 6th Airborne Brigades, another unit flanked the enemy, and the 8th Airborne Brigade in Lemi. The TRA reacted by deploying the 6th Mechanised Brigade, the 18th and 19th Infantry Brigades, the 4/82/2 and 5/82/2 Sparta Brigades, and even a tank company from the SDB to rescue the besieged paratroopers. Arriving on 23 May 1990, these managed to punch through, enabling the 5th, 6th, and 8th Airborne Brigades to break out of the encirclement, and forcing the insurgents to retreat across the Jamma River. However, this was a pyrrhic victory: although the military intelligence subsequently concluded that in only three days of fighting the insurgents had suffered 1,082 casualties, the 102nd Airborne Division of the Ethiopian Army alone lost 95 killed, 381 wounded, and staggering 2,652 soldiers missing in action – and that out of 6,421 troops with which it entered this battle. The other involved units suffered an additional loss of 729 killed, wounded and missing in action. Furthermore, the EPRDF captured two intact D-30 howitzers, four BM-24s, and two T-55 MBTs.

A group of EPLA fighters deployed inside Ethiopia, at an unknown date. (Adrien Fontanellaz Collection)

Insurgents atop a captured T-54/55 MBT in May 1990. (Adrien Fontanellaz Collection)

From Triumph into Catastrophe

Worst of all was that when one prong of the Ethiopian advance was stalled, the other was stalled too: because the 102nd Airborne Division was in such trouble, and all the available reserves were spent to rescue it, the 3rd Infantry Division was forced to stop in Degolo – and thus missed the chance to catch the insurgents in a vulnerable moment. Nevertheless, when ordered to resume its advance, this division punched through. Indeed, proving its seasoned veterans were made of better stuff than most of the Ethiopian military by that time, its 92nd Infantry Brigade executed a text-book small action while taking Karra Mesheg fortress in a night attack supported by a flanking movement on 26 May. Unsurprisingly, this attracted the wrath of the EPRDF: during the following day, the insurgents launched no less than 17 attacks in an attempt to recapture this critical position. Having repulsed all of these, the 3rd Infantry resumed its advance and took Maranna, on 29 May 1990, in the face of bitter resistance.

Precisely at this point of time, when the 3rd Infantry Division's advance was about to reach Alem Ketema and thus throw the EPRDF's dispositions into a complete chaos, the TRA ordered the division to stop – because its commanders decided to reorganise their other units before attacking this important town only during the second phase of this offensive (Operation Flame II). The 3rd Infantry Division thus not only remained at Maranna, but was reinforced by the 2nd Paracommando Brigade and the 4/82/2 Sparta Brigade, while the 4th Infantry Division was brought up into a position for an attack on Alem Ketema from the east.

Military strategists might have endless discussions whether such a reorganisation was really necessary, or not. The facts are that, in May 1990, it had offered the EPRDF – which was meanwhile on the verge of panic – an opportunity to cool down and reorganise its own units too. Over the following three days, the Ethiopian military intelligence identified the re-deployment of not only the Aurora, Awash, Agazi, Lab Adar, and May Day, but also Maebal and Maqdala Divisions into the Alem Ketema area. Therefore, instead of striking into an only poorly defended area and thus collapsing the major body of the EPRDF, Flame II was about to hit straight into the hornet's nest.

Worse yet, the insurgency was much faster with its regrouping: so much so, it launched its own offensive already at dawn on 3 June, virtually pre-empting the Flame II. By 4 June 1990, the EPRDF captured several heights along the road between Dessie and Wara Ilu, thus isolating not only the 3rd and 4th Infantry Divisions, but the 2nd Paracommando and the 4/82/2 Spara Brigades. Already exhausted by their advance, Ethiopian troops now had to be resupplied by helicopters – which often arrived loaded with new shoes and uniforms instead with food and ammunition![69] The attempt of the 10th Infantry Brigade (from the 3rd Division) to unblock the road proved unsuccessful, as did all the counterattacks by the 8th and 26th Infantry Divisions from the other side.

Finding no other solution, the TRA ordered the beleaguered troops to resume their advance on Alem Ketema – thus exposing them to countless ambushes and counter-attacks. Finally, on 11 June, the insurgents launched a massive, multi-prong counterattack in the direction of the Karra Mesheg fortress: by the evening of the next day, this site had changed hands at least twice. The TRA then ordered the 102nd Airborne Division to resume its advance too, while the 10th and 18th Infantry Brigades approached the Alem Ketema area from the direction of Lemi. Although suffering heavy losses by this time, the EPRDF was not ready to give up. On the contrary, on 15 June, it launched desperate, yet simultaneous, multi-prong attacks on nearly all Ethiopian units. The plan worked: discouraged troops fell back, leaving a trail of heavy equipment as they were forced to break out on foot across mountains in the direction of friendly positions. Their losses were devastating: even the commander of the 3rd Infantry Division, Colonel Sereke Berhan was captured after refusing to be evacuated by helicopter. By 16 June, his division virtually ceased to exist, following a loss of 2,518 troops missing, 13 T-55s, 10 D-30 howitzers, and 8 ZU-23 anti-aircraft cannons. Operation Flame, actually a highly-promising enterprise, thus turned into a staggering defeat and destruction of two crucial Ethiopian divisions.[70]

A well entrenched position of a recoilless rifle operated by the EPLA. (Adrien Fontanellaz Collection)

An insurgent-operated T-54/55 in action during the Ethiopian Army's last large-scale counteroffensive – Operation Flame – in May-June 1990. (Adrien Fontanellaz Collection)

A PKM-armed team of the EPLA in action. (Adrien Fontanellaz Collection)

As if this all was not enough, instead of providing CAS to the ground troops all through Operation Flame, the EtAF continued striking civilians in Wollo, Shewa, and Tigray. Rama, Alem Ketena, Kolesh, Ambat and Merhabete were also bombed in May; while Tenta, Wurgessa, Deha, Isitayoh, and Nefas Maucha were bombed in June 1990. Indeed, on 23 June 1990, multiple formations of fighter-bombers of the Ethiopian Air Force bombed Addi Abun for nearly 40 minutes as a large group of civilians gathered to commemorate the second anniversary of the bombing of Hausien in front of the church of Abune Teklehaimanot. The number of deaths in resulting massacres still remains unknown.[71]

Operation Tewodros

Following the disastrous end of Operation Flame, the Ethiopian Army was still in control of the vital roads linking Addis Ababa with Asseb, Dessie and Gondar. Prompted by Mengistu, the then MOND launched a major reorganisation of its remaining units, creating seven zones, with the Zone 1 covering Eritrea and Tigray, and Zone 2 Gondar and Gojam, while the Ethiopian strongman began day-dreaming about mobilising a popular militia of 500,000 to defeat the EPRDF – although his military was barely able to make up the losses of existing units.[72]

Operation Flame left deep scars in the ranks of the insurgency, too, and thus it was several months before the leadership of the EPRDF felt ready to launch a new campaign – this time with the aim of delivering the decisive blow against the Derg. Early on, insurgent strategists had studied a quite straightforward advance from Dessie on Addis Ababa. Eventually, they opted for a different plan after receiving intelligence about the MOND taking care to significantly bolster the 605th Corps, and develop a strong defence north of Debre Birhan. Ultimately, neither of these options was exercised: the EPRDF decided to first destroy the 603rd Corps and thus completely eliminate the Derg's presence in Gondar and Gojam Provinces. Codenamed Tewodros, after the Ethiopian Emperor, this operation was to be undertaken during the rainy season (between February and April 1991), when the weather was likely to ground most of the EtAF. By then, the EPRDF had been reinforced by two mechanised brigades of the EPLA, with one deployed in Gondar, and the other in the Dessie area.[73]

This Operation Tewodros was initiated on 23 February 1991, with a multi-prong attack on positions of the 603rd Corps between Bahir Dar and Werata – and was promptly crowned by success. The 33rd Infantry Brigade was quickly isolated in the Werata area. Although it managed to break out – destroying several insurgent T-55s in the process – and rally with the 154th Infantry Brigade in Addis Zemen, its withdrawal had shaken elements of the 4th Mechanised Division, which was controlling the road linking Werata with Bahir Dar. The 4th quickly collapsed into disarray and fled back towards Bahir Day, suffering extensive losses in the process – including its commander, Colonel Beruk Dajane.

Instead of retreating back into the mountains, like at earlier times, this time the EPRDF continued the advance all the way to Bahir Dar. Early on the morning of 24 February, the insurgent artillery began shelling the local air base, forcing the commander of the 4th Command, EtAF, to order a hurried evacuation of all the operational MiG-23BNs. On the next morning, the insurgents began investing Bahir Dar, causing a bitter battle that was to last until 4 March 1991, although the majority of Ethiopian Army units had already run away in direction of Bure by 26 February. Without waiting for the fall of Bahir Dar, the EPRDF then deployed its May Day and Awash Divisions for an attack in the direction of Meshenti, the major base and the main supply dump of the 603rd Corps. Although local commanders did manage to blow up most of the supply depots, once again, the Ethiopian Army's defences collapsed within hours. Furthermore, the military failed to destroy the local fuel storage – with disastrous consequences.

Now split into two parts that were isolated from each other (one still defended Gondar, the other was in full retreat towards Bure), and with most of its units in chaos, the 603rd Corps was ripe for its ultimate destruction. On 27 February 1991, another insurgent force assaulted Debre Marqos, and advanced on Bure, thus forcing the retreating military to flee in the direction of Nekemte. This dissolution of the 603rd Corps was stopped only through the deployment of the brand-new 205th Airborne Division and two other brigades, which established defensive positions at Kiremu (on the road from Bure to Nekemte), and on the bridge spanning the Blue Nile River between Debre Marqos and Addis Ababa.

An insurgent column, supported by a T-54/55 MBT, 'on advance in direction of Addis Ababa', in early 1991. (Bahir Dar War Memorial)

Indeed, by early March 1991, the MOND concentrated no fewer than 26,804 troops in this area, including not only the 205th Airborne, but also the 30th and 31st Infantry Divisions, and a battalion of the SDB supported by a company of T-62Ms. Much less successful was the series of changes of command of the 603rd Corps: Brigadier-General Abebe Haile Selassie was replaced by Brigadier-General Assefa Mossissa, who was almost immediately replaced by Brigadier-General Wassihun Nigatu.[74]

This new situation prompted the EPRDF's commanders to split their forces. While one prong continued spilling into Wellega Province, the other – reinforced by a mechanised brigade of the EPLA – concentrated for an attack on the 603rd Corps in Gondar. This operation was run in what was meanwhile the 'standard tactics' for insurgents: in the form of multiple diversionary attacks, combined with a flanking movement. The resulting battle for Gondar was bitter, as the beleaguered Ethiopian garrison – resupplied by air via the Azazo airport – continued fighting despite its hopeless position. Indeed, on 24 February 1991, the EPRDF force advancing along the Metema-Gondar road was stopped cold in an ambush set up by the 133rd Infantry Brigade, which then launched an effective counter-attack too. Similarly, the insurgent force that advanced along the road from Shire, ran into the 136th Infantry Brigade between Dabat and Amba Giorgies, and suffered heavy casualties. Only the third EPDRF prong, that approached from the direction of Werata while supported by artillery, several BM-21s, and at least 10 T-55s, did manage to punch through: despite counterattacks by the 33rd and 154th Infantry Brigades, it managed to capture Gondar on 25 February 1991. The latter force resumed its advance on 28 February, in hot pursuit of the exhausted 154th Brigade, although repeatedly hit by air strikes. It brought its artillery within range of the Azazo airport by 2 March 1991, and instantly opened fire, forcing the air force to evacuate its fighter-bombers and helicopters to Debre Zeit air base. On the same day, the fourth insurgent prong – a force that advanced from Bahir Dar along the Lake Tana – reached the Gorgora area, taking the Ethiopians by surprise.

The MOND reacted by ordering the SRA in Eritrea to deploy the 4th Infantry Division into a counterattack into Tigray, but this was defeated by a combined EPRDF/EPLA force near Adwa in

A Mi-35 helicopter gunship of the EtAF, as seen in May 1991. The Ethiopian Air Force remained the last disciplined and organized branch of the Ethiopian military, and continued fighting against the insurgent advance to the last day of the war. (Herve Dessallier via Albert Grandolini)

early March. Therefore, the insurgents continued their advance on Gondar almost undisturbed. In a last-ditch attempt to save the situation, the EtAF finally bombed the EPRDF's artillery that was shelling the Azazo airport, buying the time necessary for a single transport aircraft to land and unload supplies on 6 March. However, this was not enough: the Ethiopian Army defences crumbled, and Gondar fell on 8 March 1991.

Ultimately, Operation Tewodros thus succeeded in expelling the Derg from Gondar and Gojam Provinces in a matter of two weeks. This in turn emboldened the OLF into launching its first large-scale operation and taking the town of Gename on 21 February 1991.[75]

Pilots of No. 10 Squadron, EtAF, as seen at Dire Dawa in 1990. From left towards right, they are Belayneh Tegegn, Fanta Olana, Dawit Wondifraw, Mesfin Haile, Bahiru Gizaw, and Tilahun Bogale. (EtAF via S.N.)

Final Blows

Encouraged by the tremendous success of Operation Tewodros, the EPRDF continued exercising pressure upon the remnants of the Ethiopian Army during March 1991 too. Early in the morning of 11th March, it launched Operation Bilisumaf Walqituma ('Freedom and Equality' in Oromo) against the concentration of troops in the Kiremu area. The 31st Infantry Division collapsed almost immediately and beat a hasty retreat, thus exposing the flank of the 205th Airborne Division. In this fashion, the insurgents were able to cross the Blue Nile River. A counterattack by the 30th Infantry Division did retake some of the lost ground, but was easily outflanked by an insurgent force that established a blocking position between the river and Kiremu: the 30th Division was virtually destroyed while attempting to withdraw.

Nevertheless, its sacrifice bought the time for the army to bring in reinforcements and establish a new, corps-sized unit – ironically designated Task Force Tewodros. Commanded by Major-General Mardassa Lelissa, this controlled a total of four infantry divisions and a mechanised brigade that stabilised the situation through successful defence of the Dessie Debre Birhan axis, Debre Sina, and the Fincha hydroelectric power-plant, crucial for keeping Addis Ababa supplied with electricity. The EtAF hit back at the advancing insurgent columns heavily from the air, reportedly delivering some of its most effective air strikes of the entire war. However, these failed to change the overall situation and there was little doubt that the general position of the Derg was worsening with every hour.[76]

Indeed, after several failed attempts, the EPRDF punched through and secured the Fincha Dam by mid-April 1991, and then established a defence line from Welkite to Gohatsion, Waliso and Ambo – barely 100 kilometres from the Ethiopian capital – where it managed to repulse multiple counterattacks from the army. Better supplied and supported than ever before, the insurgents then invested the town of Ambo, on 24 April, but were repulsed by a force drawn from the SRA and including elements of the 605th Corps, supported by up to 50 air strikes.

In May 1991, the EPRDF launched Operation Walalen against seven divisions of the Ethiopian Army deployed between Dessie and Debre Birhan. Although the reconstituted 3rd Infantry Division offered its usual, excellent performance while defending the Tarmabar tunnels, eventually, the 605th Corps collapsed and Dessie fell on 18 May 1991. With this, the Derg lost its last land connection to the port of Asseb. This catastrophe happened around the same time that the insurgents finally secured Ambo, on 19 May, followed by Ginchi, a day later.

Finally realising that the situation was hopeless, on 21 May 1991 Mengistu Haile Mariam boarded the DeHavilland Canada DHC-5 with registration ET-AHJ and fled to Kenya, together with a handful of followers. From Nairobi, he continued the trip all the way to Harare in Zimbabwe on board a Boeing 707 of Kenyan Airways. As soon as this became known in Ethiopia the remaining military virtually dissolved itself and ceased offering resistance. Three columns of the EPRDF thus entered Addis Ababa on 28 May only to face some resistance from a few die-hards from the SDB entrenched in the compound of the Presidential Palace. These were overrun rather quickly. The fall of Addis Ababa thus ended the war that ravaged Ethiopia for three decades.[77]

Ethiopian Army troops captured by the EPLA. Thousands of them had spent years as prisoners of war: many were convinced to join sides of the TPLF and the EPRDF, while others remained in Eritrea. (Albert Grandolini Collection)

The TPLF-Factor

When studying the Ethiopian-Eritrean War of 1961-1991, and especially its final decade, the conclusion is unavoidable that the defeat of the forces of the Derg government was self-inflicted. The mistreatment of the military by Mengistu Haile Mariam had reached such proportions, that it not only made most of the officers and other ranks unwilling to fight for what was clearly a lost cause, but outright destroyed the Navy, followed by the Army and the Air Force. However, while the usual histories of this conflict emphasise the defeats of the Red Star Campaign and then at Afabet – i.e. the war between the Derg and the Eritrean insurgency – as events that totally demoralised the Ethiopian military, and thus caused its collapse in 1991, a closer look reveals an entirely different picture.

Quite on the contrary: while certainly keeping the Ethiopian military preoccupied for most of the 1980s, and thus indirectly shielding the TPLF while this was still gaining strength, the EPLF/EPLA not only failed to instrument the complete defeat of the Ethiopian military in Eritrea: it actually played a very limited role in Mengistu's downfall. Although certainly instrumental in breaking the morale of the Ethiopian military, and for tying down more than a third of its divisions in Eritrea, by 1991 the Eritrean insurgency alone did not represent a mortal threat for the Derg. Instead, the crucial element in this process was the emergence and growth of what was originally a small group of dedicated political opponents in Tigray.

The TPLF did not fight for the independence of that province, but to topple Mengistu and the Derg. It did not defeat the Ethiopian military by letting it assault well-entrenched positions like those of the EPLA in the Sahel Redoubt, but excelled at manoeuvring warfare, causing shock and driving Ethiopian officers into despair. Finally, the military build-up of the TPLF was extremely effective: by 1991, it had developed the most powerful conventional army in all of Africa, including 15 division-sized formations. It is striking that the leadership of the Tigrayan insurgency had prepared for such a massive and fast build-up, years in advance – indeed: since the early 1980s – and thus took great care to train its military cadre so to be able to take positions much higher than their nominal tasks. These were the elements that made this insurgency as successful as to enable an advance from Tigray all the way to Addis Ababa, and thus end what began as the war for Eritrean independence.[78]

This fact is even more important considering the TPLF managed this achievement with next to no support from abroad (except for food deliveries and a few small arms and ammunition shipments from countries such as Egypt), and with only temporary help from the EPLF: for its military equipment, this insurgency always remained heavily dependent upon arms captured from government forces.

One of the fundamental reasons for the development of such capabilities were rich Ethiopian military traditions and history, summarised in Volume 1 of this mini-series. As described in its Chapter 1, Ethiopian kings and local landlords were routinely mobilising huge armies, mixing the core of dozens of their bodyguards, with thousands of warriors, levies and militiamen. They proved capable of keeping such armies sustained even for longer periods of times, and of deploying them to wage long-range offensive operations (as the Italians had discovered already in 1896, at Adwa). Next, the TPLF profited from having thousands of its recruits trained by the EPLF at bases in its Sahel Redoubt, in the early 1980s, while the Derg de-facto ignored its rear bases in Tigray. However, the knowledge acquired through the training by the EPLF would have been useless without the leadership of the TPLF also making methodical use of lessons from other insurgencies abroad, especially that of the People's Liberation Army of China. Years of studies of Mao's teachings resulted in the Ethiopian insurgent leaders learning how to conduct even larger operations while avoiding being cornered by a superior conventional enemy.

The next crucial factor in this war was the emergence of TPLF's conventional warfare capability, strongly influenced by professional military officers that were either captured or had defected from the Derg's military. Not only that the TPLF's leadership was not too proud to let them do this: these men then proved instrumental in teaching basic military tactics to the still nascent movement, but also in helping the insurgency to master huge amounts of heavy weapons captured during the fall of Tigray, and then – drawing heavily on their military education – to outmanoeuvre and outfight the conventional military of the government. Ironically, very little is known about the officers in question and there is no doubt about a certain dose of resentments against them being existent within the ranks of Ethiopian military veterans living abroad – until this very day. One of few exceptions is Colonel Sereke Berhan, former commander of the 3rd Infantry Division, who played the crucial role in training EPRDF's mechanised units. For all practical reasons, it can thus be said, that the Derg government not only destroyed its own military, but also helped develop the military that destroyed its rule too.

Finally, the decisive role of the EPRDF as a political vehicle should not be ignored: its structure enabled the TPLF to operate well outside Tigray, and that at ease.

Overall, the essence of the TPLF – and thus the EPDRF – was a military that was self-developed. This fact alone should be always kept in mind when considering the effectiveness of several other insurgencies that emerged victorious in other conflicts in Africa of the 1980s and 1990s, but also in regards of the Ethiopian military effectiveness ever since 1991.

CHAPTER 6
POST-WAR RECONSTRUCTION

As two allies from the war against the Derg government, the EPLF-dominated transitional government of Eritrea, and TPLF/EPRDF-dominated transitional government of Ethiopia enjoyed and maintained close cooperation during the early 1990s. Amongst others, the EPRDF agreed that the EPLF should set up an autonomous transitional government in Asmara and a referendum was to be held to find out if Eritreans wanted to secede from Ethiopia or not. The referendum was held in early 1993, and in April that year Eritrea declared its independence and joined the UN.

Meanwhile, new authorities in both countries launched efforts to reorganise their militaries. To describe the resulting process as 'dramatic', would be an understatement. With propaganda being an unavoidable ingredient of every modern conflict, many legends came into being during the last years of the Derg government and afterwards, mostly superimposing the combat efficiency of the EPLA's and TPLA/EPRDF's insurgents over the incompetence of the Ethiopian military. Correspondingly, the former were famed and the latter all too easily disregarded. Rather gradually, the military leadership of the EPRDF was forced into realisation that – its military narcissism aside – it lacked all the expertise necessary to run an effective conventional military. Indeed, it realised that the critical difficulties of the Ethiopian military of the 1980s were centred upon the performance of the combat infantry: while poorly trained and led, this carried the overwhelming burden of battle, and of casualties. On the contrary, one of the greatest Derg achievements of the war was the expansion of the tiny force from the 1970s, into an army of nearly 400,000 – with the inevitable consequence of a chronic shortage of high-quality, trained career leaders. The principal problem was that there were never enough of these. Concluding they now had enough time to train, to prepare, and to plan for the future, military strategists of the EPRDF of the 1990s thus decided to return to the principle of quality over quantity. The essence of this process was to become their capability to attract former officers of the Ethiopian military that possessed excellent military education and plentiful operational experience. While never conceded publicly – partially for political reasons, but also the very obnoxious nature of the Derg Regime – and despite the outcome of many battles and the war in general, the inescapable truth was that the Ethiopian military of the 1980s included thousands of well-educated and highly efficient officers. While defecting en masse during the last days of the Derg government, and immediately afterwards, many of these subsequently returned, and then played a decisive role in the post-war reconstruction of the Ethiopian and Eritrean militaries. Ironically, the EPLF/EPLA-leadership actually drew similar conclusions. However, while initially following the Ethiopian example in regards of recruiting officers that used to serve under the Derg, the Eritrean authorities subsequently pursued their own, significantly different version of a strategy of national defences. Thus, it can be said that professional Ethiopian military officers were much sought for – and then by both governments in Addis Ababa and Asmara.

Operation Godoria

In addition to Ethiopian troops that fled from Eritrea to Sudan, as described above, more than 10,000 officers and other ranks from the 5th Mechanised, 5th Infantry, and the 22nd Mountain Infantry Divisions had entered the territory of Djibouti along the coastal road linking Asseb with Khor Angar. Other troops fled along the railway track. No less than 12 warships of the Ethiopian Navy – carrying about 4,000 sailors and members of their families – sailed for Yemen on 27 May 1991. Additional vessels were intercepted by the French Navy. Ironically, while defeated and demoralised, these troops were far more numerous – and better armed – than the miniature military of Djibouti. Thus, most had to be disarmed by the members of the 3,503-strong French garrison stationed in that country in the course of Operation Godoria. Between 26 May and 2 June 1991, the French troops seized 200 tonnes of ammunition, 13,000 firearms, about 30 armoured vehicles – including 27 T-55s and T-62s, 3 BTR-60s, and at least 1 ZSU-23-4 Shilka. Furthermore, within the fame of Operation Totem, the French Air Force evacuated about 300 expatriates from Addis Ababa.

In comparison, the majority of top EtAF officers were arrested by the insurgents during the following days. Amongst them was the last Chief-of-Staff of the air force, Major-General Alemayehu Agonafer, Brigadier-General Techane Mesfin, Deputy commander of the air force responsible for training, and even Brigadier-General Ashenafi Gebre-Tsadik, hero of the Ogaden War, released from a Somali prison only two years before. Most of them were imprisoned until September 1998.[79] Fearing prosecution, many of their subordinates decided to defect instead. The first to go was Captain Fanta Jallo, who landed his MiG-23BN at Khartoum IAP, while Captain Balaynah Tekegn and Lieutenant Mesfin flew their MiG-23BNs to Ambouli IAP, in Djibouti, on 21 May 1991. A day later, a pair of MiG-23BN pilots landed at Wajir IAP, outside Nairobi in Kenya. The mass of EtAF pilots defected only in the following days, once Debre Zeit AB was about to be overrun by the EPRDF. One of the Ethiopian MiG-21 pilots recalled how this situation developed:

'Debre Zeit was different in those days. There was a lot of gunfire at night, and the town was not what it used to be. Officers convinced the war is over went home. Others contemplated leaving, but were nervous while looking for the right moment. The Colonel [in command of the unit; authors' note] called me by rank and said, 'An operational order has just been received, and we need to fly to Dire Dawa'. Shortly before leaving, one of my friends from the Operations Cell called me to tell me that Asmara has fallen. I know that was the beginning of the end. With the Colonel in lead, we took off with our MiG-21s and headed towards Dire Dawa…

When we arrived there, the air base was packed full with aircraft from Asmara. The atmosphere was tense and everyone was watching everyone. There I found one of my friends from the childhood and he told me to stay close to him all the time…

An hour later, a helicopter arrived carrying a high-ranking officer. At first, I thought he would be running the operation from here, but I also knew, things weren't developing well and the air force could not make any difference. Less than an hour later, the high ranking officer re-emerged with another pilot: they both walked to a helicopter, took off and flew away. Everyone who witnessed the scene then decided to save his own skin. What happened next is something I do not want to remember. Regardless of the rank, everybody was grabbing whatever they could find to get out, me included. With my helicopter pilot and another pilot, we took off and headed for Djibouti. Once we arrived there, they gathered us at the terminal and then jailed us. After a week-long stay, we were handed over to the UN refugee agency. By the time, Ethiopia has fallen.'[80]

In the course of the overflight in question, the crews of four MiG-23BNs, one L-39C, four An-12Bs, one Cessna 185, six Mi-24s and Mi-35s, six Mi-8s, and two Alouette IIIs had found refuge at Ambouli IAP. Numerous aircraft of the Ethiopian Airlines were to follow, including two Boeing 707s, two Lockheed L-100 Hercules transports, two DHC-6 Twin Otters, and two Avions de Transport Régional ATR-42s.[81] Ultimately, all of these – and most of their crews and civilians that arrived on board them – were returned to Ethiopia, as described by the same source:

'It was June 1991 and the Djibouti-heat is hell. It was completely unbearable in the refugee camp, but there was no choice. That was the life as a refugee. While at the camp, a pilot who was also my course-mate came to the idea of going back to Debre Zeit. After a few days of talking, four pilots – including me – decided to leave the camp, and take a train back to Ethiopia. As I wasn't sure how things might turn out, I decided to get off at Dire Dawa, then wait there and see. I knew an old friend in that town and stayed with him and his family. The others continued their journey to Debre Zeit.

Few weeks later, I received a phone message. It was one of the pilot who travelled with us from Djibouti and continued all the way to Debre Zeit. He asked me to return to the air force. I still wasn't sure and I asked him what guarantees for my safety I've had. He angrily replied, 'except for you, everyone is returning to their job'. A heated exchange ensued, after which he issued an ultimatum: 'Are you coming or not? If you are, a helicopter will be sent to pick you up.' I knew him since longer but was still surprised when he offered to send me a helicopter. This meant the things could not be that bad. Thus, I told him I was willing to return. Indeed, an Alouette helicopter was then sent to Dire Dawa AB to pick me up. That's how I joined the TPLF's air force.

The situation at Debre Zeit of those days was shocking for me. Like a horrible dream. Pilots and technicians were returning to work, but it didn't seem that anybody was in charge of the base. Officers' quarters were converted to living quarters and Sudanese Antonovs were hauling in cargo we had no idea about…

A row of two Ethiopian An-12Bs and one An-26 that landed at Ambouli IAP, in Djibouti, on 24 May 1991. (Herve Dessalier via Albert Grandolini)

One of four MiG-23BNs flown to Ambouli IAP at Djibouti was this example, serial number 1266. Notable is that it already wore the new camouflage pattern, including much darker colours – applied during the overhaul in Ethiopia. (Herve Dessalier via Albert Grandolini)

The sole L-39C evacuated to Ambouli IAP was this example, with the serial number 1709. The aircraft was wearing the same camouflage pattern as applied prior to delivery. (Herve Dessalier via Albert Grandolini)

This Cessna 185 of the former Army Aviation Battalion, then the 6th Command EtAF, was the only aircraft of that type evacuated to Djibouti in May 1991. (Herve Dessalier via Albert Grandolini)

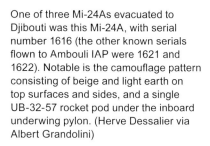

One of three Mi-24As evacuated to Djibouti was this Mi-24A, with serial number 1616 (the other known serials flown to Ambouli IAP were 1621 and 1622). Notable is the camouflage pattern consisting of beige and light earth on top surfaces and sides, and a single UB-32-57 rocket pod under the inboard underwing pylon. (Herve Dessalier via Albert Grandolini)

Amongst the three Mi-35s flown to Ambouli IAP was this example, with serial number 2015. Like all the other Ethiopian aircraft and helicopters, it was subsequently flown back to Ethiopia and re-entered service with the re-established air force. (Herve Dessalier via Albert Grandolini)

No fewer than six Mi-8Ts of the 6th Command, EtAF were evacuated to Djibouti, in May 1990. This example wore the serial 857. (Herve Dessalier via Albert Grandolini)

Slow Recovery

After the fall of the Derg government in May 1991, the military of the EPRDF became Ethiopia's official military force. While set up to meet the political objectives of the Front, and certainly reaching a high level of conventional fighting capability, the insurgency was neither trained nor able to function as a regular army: it lacked a mass of capabilities necessary to perform such tasks. Furthermore, not only the military wing of the EPRDF, but also what was left of the former Ethiopian military was too large for the new government to support. Initially at least, the new Ethiopian government was not being curious to merge its own with the former military, as commented by Yemane Kidane, Chief of Personnel and Administration at the Ministry of National Defence as of the early 1990s:

> Appointing officers of the Derg Army to command positions would have been a recipe for disaster. ... Our objective was to create a totally new army, in contrast to South Africa where what you have is a kind of half-breed army in which the old army still influences the new one.[82]

This meant that the existing military had to be demobilised. Run under the control of the Commission for the rehabilitation of the Members of the Former Army and Disabled War Veterans, the related process was massive: it resulted in about 455,000 military persons – including 38,000 disabled – being disarmed, and undergoing political re-education courses before being sent home. Over 100,000 former insurgents were to follow in the process that proved slightly more problematic than expected because some of members of the EPRDF continued mobilising. For example, the Oromo Liberation Front continued expanding its military wing from 5,000 to 25,000 between May 1991 and mid-1992. It was only on a direct order (and some threats) from Addis Ababa, that 21,000 of these were demobilised. Similarly, the demobilisation of the EPRDF was quite slow: it was only by 1995 that about 30,000 of its combatants were demobilised – and then because the new government was keen to bring the defence budget to a sustainable level of 2.3% of the Gross Domestic Product.

In turn, the government began developing a detailed plan for a complete reform and the establishment of a new military. Reaching back upon experiences from the creation and the build-up of the TPLF, the decision was taken to first create the core of the new Ethiopian National Defence Force (ENDF) as a professional military force of about 54,000, and then develop the capability for further growth through training the cadre to assume responsibilities above their ranks. The new military was to put great emphasis on COIN warfare – a requirement proved correct when the OLF re-launched its insurgency in 1993 – but also be able of quickly expanding in case of a conventional war with one of their neighbours, through the establishment of a large and adequately trained reserve force. It was at this point that the ENDF had concluded that it needed the expertise of officers and other ranks of what was still generally considered the 'Derg army'. Correspondingly, the decision was taken to retain about 7,000 of these – including some 2,000 from the EtAF – primarily because of their technical expertise. Unsurprisingly, the ENDF had developed a set of stringent criteria about whom to retain and whom not:

emphasis was put on low to mid-ranking officers that were fully-qualified technical specialists, and had no history of serving as political commissars or members of the former security structure. Foremost sought for were Colonels with good military education, extensive combat and operational experiences: they were put in charge of emerging training centres and the future logistics system.

Officially at least, the ENDF came into being following the adoption of a new Constitution in 1995, when it was defined as including an army, an air force, and the defence industry, the work of which was coordinated by the National Defence Council – chaired by the Chief-of-Staff Army. In turn, the Chief of Staff was responsible to the Minister of National Defence. Along with the same reform, the military established three commands: the Northern, Eastern and South-Western. By the time, about 15,000 new troops from all parts of the country were recruited, enabling an expansion of all the existing brigades into divisions. Correspondingly, each of the newly-established commands headquarters was assigned two divisions, each of which in turn consisted of one infantry brigade, one commando brigade, and one mechanised brigade. Finally, a separate mechanised division was established as a strategic reserve and a 'pool' for reinforcing other formations as necessary. This large unit had an armoured brigade with about 75-100 tanks; an artillery brigade with 57 guns; an air defence brigade, an anti-tank brigade, a commando brigade, and a motorised infantry brigade.[83]

Rebuilding the Air Force

Although the leadership of the EPRDF was quick in recognizing the importance of air power and in resurrecting the flying service under the official title 'Federal Democratic Republic of Ethiopia Air Force' (FDREAF, but 'Ethiopian Air Force', EtAF, remains in colloquial use), the re-building process was marred by multiple problems related as much to the efforts of the former insurgents to install their cadre into all important positions, as the refusal of some of officers that used to serve under the Derg to accept the new realities in Ethiopia of the 1990s.

At first, the EPRDF subjected all officers and other ranks of the former air force to a re-education campaign run in so-called 'rehabilitation camps'. A group of about 50 of these were then used to return aircraft flown out to neighbouring countries, and reactivate the transport wing. Simultaneously, the EPRDF appointed six of its own military commanders into key positions in the air force, sent others for staff training abroad, and then re-launched flight training with the intention of converting a number of its seasoned combatants into pilots and ground personnel. Correspondingly, Major-General Abebe Tekle Haimanot – one of the most experienced insurgent leaders – was appointed the Chief-of-Staff EtAF, while the PTS and the MTC – meanwhile almost exclusively staffed by former officers of the EtAF – were re-opened at Bole IAP in August 1992.[84] However, the re-training of former insurgents into pilots proved anything other than easy, even more so because many of the re-commissioned officers still had quite strong anti-TPLF resentments. The above-cited former MiG-21 pilot recalled:

> 'After a while, it became obvious that the TPLF wanted us all back – and badly: they wanted us to train their own pilots. They brought seven trainees said to have been recruited from

the cross-section of the population. It was just a cover. They were all TPLF, and most did not meet any air force standards. Nevertheless, we all went straight to work. Then they brought in the second and the third batch. The third batch was different: it included people who would become the worst foes of the new government.'

Eventually, only two officers with TPLF-backgrounds completed their courses and qualified as pilots, despite a considerable investment of time and effort. Actually, the EPRDF government knew that the Ethiopian military was always a melting pot of diverse ethnic groups. Its air force was no exception, and thus included not only Amharas and members of other Ethiopian ethnic groups, but numerous Eritreans and Tigrayans too. However, facing immense financial problems while rebuilding the country, it was forced to massively decrease annual defence spending and thus downsize and streamline the air force, while bolstering its support infrastructure and making the service less dependent on support from abroad.[85]

A poor, but important photograph showing the first group of ex-EtAF instructor pilots that trained new students on L-39s, at Bole IAP, starting in August 1992. Standing, from left to right: Daniel Beyene, Fanta Olana, Bezabih Petros, Gebre Haile-Selassie, and Demelash Mekonen. (EtAF via S.N.)

Project DAVEC: A Domestic Maintenance Solution

The extent to which former EtAF officers and other ranks were actually influential in the resurrected air force became obvious in the course of the project originally designated the 'Dejen Aviation Maintenance and Engineering Complex' (DAVEC). Under conditions of experiencing constantly increasing problems with the maintenance of its aircraft and helicopters of Soviet origin, in the late 1980s the MOND and the EtAF launched the DAVEC with the help of credits for civilian purposes that Moscow had already granted to Addis Ababa. Going off track following the unsuccessful coup of 1989, Project DAVEC was subsequently re-launched and further expanded. Initially limited to the manufacture of diverse spares for MiG-21s and MiG-23s, engineers of the DAVEC began introducing several modifications to EtAF MiGs during the mid-1990s, including making their fuel systems more reliable and efficient, and then through the installation of sophisticated chaff and flare dispensers of Western design, and the addition of Taiwanese-made GPS-receivers to navigational and attack platforms of most of the available combat aircraft.[86]

Meanwhile, the Engineering Division of the ENDF and the Defence Force Engineering College began training additional technicians. The cumulative results of all the related efforts became the Aviation Maintenance and Engineering Centre, established at Debre Zeit. Officially opened only in 2003, this facility had become capable of running complex overhauls of all types of aircraft and helicopters in service with the EtAF already by the mid-1990s. Ever since, it has provided services to a number of foreign customers.[87]

Furthermore, in 1994, the EtAF re-opened its Flight School at Dire Dawa AB, re-introducing the same, rigorous, high-standard training in four phases, that ran until 1991. Basic training was still undertaken on SIAI-Marchetti SF.260s, while jet training was run on L-39s. A year later, the first batch of MiG-23BNs overhauled by the DAVEC was pressed into service at the re-established Bahir Dar AB. In 1996, the USA entered military cooperation with Ethiopia and donated four Lockheed C-130B Hercules transports. The first two were refurbished and delivered in early 1998; however, the second two were still undergoing overhauls when the Badme War erupted, and were diverted to other countries. Overall, by 1998, the general condition, status and the organisation of the EtAF was roughly back to that of the mid-1970s.[88]

This partially disassembled MiG-23BN was photographed while undergoing maintenance at the DAVEC complex in the late 1990s. (Pit Weinert Collection)

Militarisation of Eritrea

In Eritrea after the end of the war in 1991, the EPLF renamed itself into the People's Front for Democracy and Justice (PFDJ), and constituted itself as the Provisional Government of Eritrea, with its General Secretary, Isayas Afewerki as Provisional President. The EPLA was neither disbanded nor demilitarised or reformed, but became the centrepiece of a state-building concept based on a comprehensive reform of the whole of Eritrean society. For the next few years, all of its major ground units remained the same as already existed since the early 1980s: their essence changed only in so far that the personnel of these divisions was transformed into the professional army – the Eritrean Defence Force (ERDF) – which, in the case of emergency, could be rapidly expanded through recalls of reservists and addition of local militia forces. Initially at least, the ERDF took over the tasks of the police too.[89] Correspondingly, with the exception of a few that were arrested or had left the service on their own, in 1991, most of the ERDF's commanders remained in their positions because the sheer nature of the EPLF and its ideology favoured the maintenance of a relatively stable 'class' of top military commanders, and a strict separation of these from lower ranking officers. In order to maintain the semblance of egalitarianism, the Eritreans did not introduce any military ranks until 1996-1997.[90]

The general condition of the ERDF, minimal payment and poor living condition, but also a decree issued by Afewerki along which the tours of duty of all the members of the armed forces were expanded for another two years without any payment, caused a military mutiny in 1993. While not intending to topple the government, a large group of officers occupied the Asmara air base and airport, and demanded negotiations with the president. The mutiny was put down through an intervention of loyal troops and negotiations. Nevertheless, over 100 leaders were subsequently arrested and sentenced to long prison terms. Furthermore, Afewerki dismissed his Minister of Defence, Petros Solomon, and re-positioned a number of other top officers into civilian functions. Finally, he did launch a reform of the ERDF: while the two specialised divisions were expanded, all the other units of that format were down-sized to brigades, and their brigades to battalions. As a result of this downsizing, the ERDF demobilised 22,000 of its officers and other ranks during the same year, another 26,000 in 1994, about 6,000 in 1995, and a few hundred in 1996.[91]

Nevertheless, the Eritrean government subsequently intensified its policy of militarisation of the state. Compulsory national service was expanded to include all citizens – male and female – between 18 and 50 years of age, and was rigorously enforced. While the professional part of the ERDF was decreased to about 46,000 active officers and other ranks (about 30,000 of these in the ground forces, of whom only a few were females, and even fewer Muslims), most recruits had served in militias, which maintained up to 200,000 under arms. The structure of the ERDF as of 1998 was thus as presented in Table 8.

The resulting expenditures thus not only remained extremely high – placing a heavy burden upon the economy, and causing rising inflation – but the military of Eritrea became omnipresent in the public life. Most of its top officers also served as members of the Central Committee of the ruling PFDJ, and of the formal legislative, the National Assembly (where the military

is granted 10% of the seats). Commanders of Operational Zones of the Eritrean military had higher authorizations than civilian authorities in the same areas, while most mayors of different cities and towns were active military officers. Furthermore, the Eritrean military began taking control over ever larger segments of the economy. For example, while the government helped re-integrate troops demobilised in the period 1993-1996 into civilian life through comprehensive educational programmes, and through helping them establish a large number of small enterprises all over the country (like restaurants, food factories, and transport enterprises), they continued serving as reservists and could be recalled at any time. Their replacements were meanwhile trained at local military educational facilities, including an Army Training Centre in Decamare, the Flight School at Asmara IAP, and a Marine College in Massawa, while the EPLA's training centre in Sawa was expanded into a Military Academy. According to official sources, no less than 80,000 recruits underwent an education at these institutions by 1996, a further 16,000 in 1997, and 19,000 by March 1998.[92]

Table 8: ERDF Order of Battle, 1998

Unit	Commander
161 Division	Filipos Woldeyohannes
271 Division	Teklay Habteselassie
381 Division	Umer Hassan 'Tewil'
471 Division	Haile Samuel 'China'
525 Division	
2000 Division	Gerezgiher Andemariam 'Wuchu'

Despite significant amounts of aid provided from abroad, a lot of post-war reconstruction work in Eritrea after the end of the Liberation War in 1991 was undertaken by the locals. The same was valid for plenty of military equipment left behind by the withdrawing Ethiopians. Here a female welder at work. (Photo by Dan Connell)

Eritrean Air Force

Due to the lack of specialised personnel, equipment and funding, the development of the two other primary branches of the Eritrean military came forward rather slowly. While very little is known about the Eritrean Navy, and this service did not play an active role in the Badme War, a lot of details became available about the Eritrean Air Force (ERAF).

During the liberation of 1991, the EPLF found a number of unserviceable aircraft left behind by the EtAF. These included at least five MiG-23BNs (three of which were wrecked), one MiG-23ML, five MiG-21bis, two MiG-21Rs, one Northrop F-5A Freedom Fighter and four North American F-86F Sabres, five Lockheed T-33As, two Mi-17s, two Mi-24s, and one Fairchild C-119 Boxcar transport. However, not only had the US-made aircraft all been grounded since the late 1970s and early 1980s, and meanwhile become derelict, but the majority of Soviet-made aircraft were in poor condition too. Although the Eritreans found the military installations at Asmara, Massawa, and Asseb – including workshops, ammunition, fuel and depots for spare parts – in good condition, they had no personnel of their own qualified to put all of that to use.

Correspondingly, after the collapse of the Derg, the EPLF was quick to recruit a group of about a dozen former pilots, and similar-sized group of technicians and weapons specialists of the EtAF. While some – like Habtesion Hadgu, former MiG-23 pilot that defected to Yemen while flying an L-39, in April 1991 – were Eritreans, others were Ethiopians with different ethnic backgrounds.[93] The latter included Abraham Oqbgasellassie (former F-5 pilot), and Kinde Damte, who were hired with four times the salary that they used to be paid by the EtAF. The men in question helped return three combat aircraft – one MiG-21bis, one Mig-21R and a MiG-23BN – to operational condition, and flew them for the first time on 1 September 1991, which can be considered as the date on which the work to establish the ERAF began in earnest.[94]

Around the same time, Libya donated 200 R-60MK (ASCC code AA-8 Aphid) short-range air-to-air missiles (possibly some spare parts, too), to help the Eritrean attempts to return the sole MiG-23ML interceptor found at Asseb airport to service. However, related efforts were abandoned, and the R-60s proved as useless as stocks of R-13M missiles captured at Asmara in 1991: most were manufactured in the late 1970s, and meanwhile were out of their shelf-life.[95]

The ERAF was officially established during the EPLA's reorganisation into the ERDF, in 1993, with Habtesion Hadgu as the Chief-of-Staff in the rank of Brigadier-General. The first five newly recruited Eritrean pilots, including one female, began their basic training in late 1994, at Asmara IAP. This was undertaken with the help of the same group of ex-EtAF pilots serving as instructors, and on four Valmet L-90TP Redigo trainers acquired from Finland. During the Farnborough aerospace salon in 1996, Eritrea placed an order for four Aermacchi MB.339C (also cited as MB.339CE or MB.339FD) from Italy. The pilots for these were trained at Venegono (Varese), the home of the manufacturer. The first two were delivered on 8 April 1997, while the other two followed in May of the same year.[96]

Reportedly disappointed with the quality of services provided by the Italians, Hadgu prompted the government in Asmara to reach an agreement with the government in Addis Ababa and have his first five students put through two phase of basic training and fighter jet training by the Ethiopian Airlines and then the Ethiopian Air Force, at Dire Dawa AB, in Ethiopia. Although the female student was washed out in the process (she later became the first Eritrean helicopter pilot), the other four completed their courses successfully. Indeed, the Ethiopians went as far as to provide three groups of their instructors to the ERAF – each of which remained in Eritrea for six months – and these had successfully trained eight additional Eritrean pilots by April 1998. Through all of this time, the original cadre of ex-EtAF pilots and ground personnel continued serving as the backbone of the nascent air force. Furthermore, additional Eritrean cadets were still undergoing training at the PTC and the MTC until May 1998.[97]

Meanwhile, additional new aircraft were acquired in the form of four Harbin Y-12 light transports purchased in China, four Mi-8 helicopters borrowed from Ethiopia, and five Mil Mi-17s acquired from Russia. Finally, impressed by the type he saw during his training in the former USSR, Hadgu persuaded the government to place an order for 12 single-seat MiG-29s and one two-seat MiG-29UB from the Ukraine. Overall, as a result of all the training and acquisitions, the ERAF of 1998 was closely reminiscent of the EtAF of the 1970s, and organised into numbered squadrons, all of which were based at Asmara, as described in Table 9.

Table 9: ERAF Order of Battle, 1998

Unit	Aircraft Type	Tasks & Notes
No. 1 Squadron	Westwind 11258P & CL-601	VIP transport, under direct control of the government
No. 2 Squadron	L-90TP Redigo	basic training
No. 3 Squadron	Mi-8	heliborne transport and assault
No. 4 Squadron	MB.339CE/FD	advanced training and light attack
No. 5 Squadron	MiG-29, MiG-29UB	fighter-bombers and interceptors
No. 7 Squadron	Bell 412	liaison and MEDEVAC
No. 8 Squadron	Y-12	light transport

One of several EtAF MiG-21bis' left behind at Asmara and captured by the EPLA in May 1991, was this example, with serial number 1082. At least two such aircraft were subsequently repaired and pressed into service with the newly-established ERAF. (Roberto Gentilli, via Pit Weinert)

This ex-Ethiopian MiG-23BN was also captured at Asmara in May 1991. Although it received some fresh paint, Eritrean national markings and ERAF serial number ER-01 (and the nickname 'Lilo'), it was never made operational again. (Photo by Roberto Gentilli, via Pit Weinert)

A rare photograph of the only two ex-Ethiopian MiG-21bis' to be made operational and flown by the ERAF as of September 1991. In front is the MiG-21R with the serial number ER-101, with MiG-21bis ER-102 to the rear. (Photo by Roberto Gentilli, vi Pit Weinert)

A row of four MB.339s as seen at Asmara, soon after delivery in early 1998. (Photo by Roberto Gentilli)

One of four Chinese-made Y-12 light transports (serial number 802), operated by No. 8 Squadron ERAF. (Photo by Roberto Gentilli)

Eritrea acquired four Valmet L-90TP Redigos from Finland in the mid-1990s. They have served as basic trainers ever since. Their original livery was replaced by a camouflage pattern during the Badme War. (Photo by Roberto Gentilli)

CHAPTER 7
BADME WAR, 1998-2001

Relations between Eritrea and Ethiopia initially after the end of the war in 1991, and following Eritrean independence of 1993, were cordial. Although Eritrea got nearly exclusive control over Ethiopia's access to the sea, the government in Asmara guaranteed that Ethiopia could use the port of Asseb on the same terms as Eritrea. Eritrea retained the Ethiopian currency, and the trade between the two countries boomed. The first differences emerged in 1997, when Eritrea introduced its own currency, the Naqfa. Contrary to what the government in Asmara expected, this act – nominally necessary to implement its own monetary policy – found little sympathy in Ethiopia, where the government prohibited a free circulation of the new Eritrean currency for anything other than small, local trading. While causing some damage to the Eritrean economy, this measure was foremost a slap in the face of the Eritrean President Afewerki, who considered himself in a position of strongly influencing the decision-making processes in Addis Ababa. In reaction, he made the issue of cross-

border trade regulation, the control of the borders, and of their exact position, a matter of importance. Correspondingly, a Joint Committee was set up to try to resolve diverse disputes. The principal issue became the line of the border: on the independence of Eritrea, the two governments reached an agreement that they would adhere to the borders that were in existence at the time the Derg collapsed. The Badme region remained under Ethiopian administration: in 1993 three local elections had taken place under regional and international supervision, and – amongst others – the region elected its representative in the Ethiopian Parliament. Eritrea never complained about such elections, or any other activities of the Ethiopian administration. However, by 1997, Afewerki – in attempt to enhance his reputation at home and help maintain Eritrea's privileged economic relationship with Ethiopia – decided to claim the Badme region for Eritrea.[98]

Following a series of small-scale armed incidents that occurred between Eritrean military and Ethiopian militia and police patrols in the Badme area between 6 and 8 May 1998, the Eritreans launched an undeclared war on Ethiopia, in the form of an invasion of the area in question. At 0530 of 12 May 1998, at least two regular brigades of the ERDF, supported by tanks and artillery, attacked the Badme area. Facing merely poorly armed militia and some police, later the same day, and on 13 May, the Eritrean armed forces then pushed across the Badme plain to higher ground in the east, and seized several border areas in Ethiopia's Tahtay Adiabo Wereda, and two places in the neighbouring Laelay Adiabo Wereda – all of which are within undisputed Ethiopian territory.[99]

Initially unprepared, indeed shocked by such behaviour, the government in Addis Ababa needed nearly a week to react. It announced a general mobilisation only on 13 May 1998. As the Eritreans deployed additional forces to secure their control of not only the Badme region, but nearby areas inside Ethiopia, the ENDF had nothing else to counter their advance but light forces equipped with fire-arms only. It was only during June 1998 that the Ethiopian military managed to create a frontline and took up defensive positions to prevent any further Eritrean advance. However, shortly after occupying the Badme region, the ERDF crossed the Mereb River further east and invaded and occupied the Mereb Lekhe Wereda area. Furthermore, in June 1998, Eritrean forces invaded Gulomakheda Wereda, including the important border town of Zalambeassa, on the road from Asmara to Addis Ababa, where they established extensive field fortifications.[100]

There followed a lull of several months, primarily conditioned by the rainy season (mid-June to mid-September), but also characterised by intensive diplomatic activities and attempts to prevent an escalation of the war. Both sides exploited this opportunity to mobilise additional forces and construct an elaborate system of fortifications along the emerging frontlines. When Eritrea refused to accept a peace plan developed by the USA and Rwanda, in February 1999 Ethiopia launched its Operation Sunset, in the course of which it regained control over virtually all of the territory occupied by Eritrea during its initial attack. In March 1999, intensive fighting erupted in the Zalambessa area, during which the Eritreans managed to hold their ground until the next rainy season stopped further operations, in June 1999. Finally, in May 2000, Ethiopia launched two final offensives of the war. During the first, it broke the back of the Eritrean military, and seized numerous towns up to 20 kilometres north of the border. During the second, Ethiopians recaptured Zalambessa and advanced on the Eritrean border town Tserona, thus pushing Eritrean forces out of Ethiopia, before seizing nearly a quarter of Eritrea and entrenching themselves well inside. Addis Ababa then declared the war as over and re-launched diplomatic efforts to end the conflict.[101]

Eritrean Assault

As of April-May 1998, most of the Ethiopian military was deployed along the border to Somalia, where an extremely destructive civil war had been going on since the 1980s. With Addis Ababa expecting no armed conflict with its northern neighbour, and the border to Eritrea being considered 'free' – any citizens of either state could cross as and when they liked, requiring only an identification card to do so – there were no ENDF units deployed anywhere in northern Tigray: only the local police

was present in the Badme area.[102] On the contrary, the ERDF was meanwhile in excellent position to fight a war. Between January and April 1998, it recalled all of its reservists – officially with an explanation of planning a major campaign of economic development.[103] The professional army of 40,000 regular troops was thus expanded through 105,000 well-trained reservists and all the existing brigades were expanded into divisions. Thus, by late May 1998, the ERDF totalled 16 divisions organised into five corps. Most units in question were former ERDF brigades, but some were newly-established: perhaps the best example was the 23rd Division, which was a combined, tank and artillery-unit. The top Eritrean military commander was meanwhile Chief-of-Staff ERDF, Major-General Uqbe Abraha, who supervised three front-commands: West (commanded by Major-General Filipos Woldejohannes), Centre (commanded by Major-General Gerezgiher Andemariam 'Wuchu'), and East (Major-General Haile Samuel 'China'). Each of the respective commanders was reporting directly to Afewerki, which caused significant problems within the command structure – because the President soon began meddling in operations-related issues without consulting his Minister of Defence or the Chief-of-Staff.[104]

On 6 May 1998, a group of Eritrean soldiers wanted to cross the border into Ethiopia at Sheraro in the direction of Badme. The Ethiopian border guards requested them to leave their arms on the border, as usual. The Eritreans refused, instead provoking a shoot-out in which several were killed on both sides. Immediately afterwards, an entire mechanised brigade of the ERDF entered the Badme region and captured the town.[105] Two days later, the joint commission for border-related issues met in Addis Ababa and agreed that the problem should be solved bilaterally, by elders of both sides, or – should that effort fail – either international intermediaries or courts were to be consulted. This process was expected to be completed within two months. Officially at least, the government in Asmara agreed to withdraw its troops from the Badme region. However, in reality it continued pouring troops into the disputed zone: by 12 May 1998, three full brigades – each some 3,000-strong and supported by about a dozen T-55 MBTs – had established themselves in the form of a triangular position west, south and east of Badme, well inside territories that were always in Ethiopia.

On 13 May 1998 Addis Ababa announced the mobilisation of its military and rushed all the available units from the border with Somalia towards north.[106] Nevertheless, it took the surprised ENDF weeks to deploy along the border to Eritrea. Meanwhile, the Ethiopian government reinforced its diplomatic activity and expressed its readiness to work with mediation from the USA and Rwanda. Indeed, a team of US and Rwandan officials arrived in Addis Ababa on 17 May, and produced a set of proposals which Ethiopia accepted on 3 June 1998. While officially negotiating, the Eritreans exploited the opportunity to widen the war: advancing along four prongs, they further reinforced their positions south of Badme, and then heavily mined all the approaches.[107] Furthermore, they captured the border village of Alitena, on 30 May, and the nearby Zalambessa, on 3 June, and finally launched an attack in the direction of Bure, in the Afar region of north-eastern region of Ethiopia. Underway, they either forcefully displaced from, or scared over 300,000 Ethiopian civilians into fleeing, their homes.[108]

Eritrean units advancing into the disputed Badme area, and into northern Ethiopia were reasonably well-supported – amongst others by about a dozen 2S1 Gvozdika self-propelled 122mm howitzers. (Mark Lepko Collection)

Infantry of the Eritrean Defence Force on the advance, close to the border to Ethiopia. (ERDF)

Camp for displaced civilians in the Barka area. (Photo by Dan Connell)

Ethiopian Counter-Strike

By this point in time, the first brigades of the ENDF were already on the frontlines. Furthermore, the EtAF had forward deployed numerous helicopters and most MiG-21bis' of its No. 20 'Cheetah' Squadron at Mekelle airport. Although only 200 kilometres from Asmara, and thus quite exposed, this base became the main hub for aerial operations against Eritrea. No. 20 Squadron was soon reinforced through deployment of at least eight MiG-23BNs from Bahir Dar. Once everything was in place, and following

the standard doctrine for situations of this kind, the air force first attempted to establish air superiority by striking the enemy's major air base. On 5 June 1998, four MiG-23BNs launched an attack on the military side of Asmara IAP – ERAF's major base. The second element aborted shortly after take off when one of the aircraft developed mechanical problems, but the first pair reached its target unmolested, hitting the workshops and killing several mechanics in the process. One of their bombs hit the main staff area, but failed to explode – thus failing to kill most of the top ERAF officers. Eritrean claims of damage on the civilian side of Asmara IAP proved wildly exaggerated: there was none. Similar can be concluded about Asmara's claims that one of the MiG-23BNs was shot down: all four jets returned safely to Mekelle.[109]

Narrowly avoiding death, an enraged Brigadier-General Hadgu ordered a counter-strike on Mekelle by all four MB.339s – colloquially known as the 'Macchis' – each flown by a single pilot. The first of the Macchis carried no bombs: it attacked the local airport at 1445 local time, deploying its internal cannon to cause some damage to a MiG-23BN and an Mi-8 (both were repaired within hours). The other three aircraft were armed with two CBUs each, and they flew in a western direction before turning for Mekelle, in order to approach the target zone out of the sun. In this way, all the Eritrean fighter-bombers passed over the centre of the Ethiopian town before reaching their target – the local airport. The second MB.339 encountered no opposition and released two bombs near the runway at 1530. However, instead of targeting Ethiopian air defences north-west of the airfield, the third Macchi dropped two CBUs on the Ayder School in the most crowded part of Mekelle, at 1700 hrs, killing 53 civilians (including 12 school children), and wounding 185 (including 42 school children). Finally, the fourth MB.339 first dropped one cluster bomb on the same Ayder neighbourhood as the third one, and then released its second bomb over an unknown area.[110] At least one MiG-21bis' armed with R-13M and R-60Mk air-to-air missiles was scrambled to intercept, but all the Eritreans descended to a very low level and thus managed to return safely to Asmara.[111]

Alarmed by massive civilian casualties in Tigray, the government in Addis Ababa – most of members of which were Tigrayans – ordered the EtAF to destroy the ERAF. Aware of the Eritrean order for MiG-29s, but knowing that these have not yet arrived, commanders at Mekelle AB hatched a much more sophisticated plan for a series of successive raids on the military side of Asmara IAP. However, Hadgu and his colleagues had anticipated such a decision: while the Ethiopian technicians worked hard through the night to prepare MiG-21s and MiG-23s for the mission, the Eritreans towed all of their aircraft into nearby bushes, and camouflaged them heavily. Instead, a few derelict MiG-21s were positioned on the tarmac – and multiple ZU-23 anti-aircraft cannons nearby.

Early on the morning of 6 June 1998, the first wave of Ethiopian fighter-bombers – four MiG-21s loaded with FAB-250M-62 bombs, led by Colonel Bezabih Petros – was detected while approaching the Eritrean capital, and the airport of Asmara was promptly evacuated. Once over the target, Petros was unable to release his ordnance. His wingman and the other two members of the formation did so, nevertheless. Petros then broke all the rules of engagement: for unknown reasons, he left his formation return to Mekelle, while turning around and deciding to attack again. Indeed, due to the same switch-failure, he failed to release his bombs on the second attempt, turned around and attacked for the third time: his bombs hit one of the hangars and caused additional damage to workshops – but in return his aircraft was hit by Eritrean flak. Petros directed his aircraft towards the road for Mendefera, but the damage precluded him from attempting an emergency landing there. He ejected over the recreation park at Adim-Zemet, near Adi Guadad. Coming down on a hill covered by trees he broke both of his legs and was found and captured by a group of local farmers a few minutes later. Bezabih Petros thus ended as a prisoner of war in Ethiopia for the second time.[112]

Following this loss, though also in an attempt to enable an evacuation of foreign citizens with the help of several chartered airliners, the Ethiopian offensive on Asmara IAP was cancelled. Indeed, Addis Ababa declared a unilateral moratorium on its own air strikes. On the ground, the Eritreans quite easily repulsed the first few Ethiopian counterattacks and continued their advance through an attempt to assault the town of Adigrat, defended by one of the first ENDF brigades that arrived on the frontlines, and the local militia and police. While the Ethiopians did manage to stop the Eritrean advance, their own counterattacks in the Badme and Tsorona regions were rather easily repulsed by Eritrean ground troops, supported by MB.339s and Mi-8s.

On 6 June 1998, one of the Macchis was claimed as shot down about 40 kilometres north of Mekelle: supposedly, the pilot ejected safely and was recovered by one of the ERAF's helicopters. However, no evidence for such a loss was ever provided, and several post-war photographs of the military side of Asmara airport show all four MB.339s still in place. Certainly enough, Ethiopian MiG-21bis' flew intensive combat air patrols along the border, but with the EtAF's poor radar coverage over the area north of Mekelle, and the rugged terrain, they never caught any of the marauding Eritreans.

On 9 June, the Ethiopians launched their first large-scale counterattack on Zalambessa, and Addis Ababa even claimed the recovery of this town. Actually, the place was meanwhile heavily fortified and the ENDF brigade deployed there was hit by fire from BM-21 MRLS and even several air strikes by MB.339s, which forced it to fall back several kilometres. On 11 June, one of the Eritrean Macchis bombed Adigrat, destroying a grain silo and killing at least four people. A day later the same town was hit by two ERAF Mi-17 helicopters. This time, they missed their main target – the local military base and the nearby pharmaceutical company – but caused considerable damage to housing and multiple civilian casualties.[113]

By that time, Ethiopian helicopters appeared over the battlefield too: Mi-8s and Mi-17s were hauling reinforcements and supplies to the frontlines, while Mi-24s and Mi-35s – meanwhile forward deployed at Axum airport, which became the home-base of the unit that operated them, known only as 'Tiger Hunter Squadron' – provided most of the CAS for ground troops, all of these flown with the assistance of forward air controllers.[114] The fighting was still heating up when a US-negotiated cease-fire agreement was reached, on 14 June 1998.

Eritrean civilians cheering next to the wreckage of Bezabih Petros' MiG-21bis serial number 1083, shot down during the air strike on Asmara Airport on 6 June 1998. (ERDF)

A column of the Ethiopian Army during a break while on a march towards the frontlines. As usual, nearly every vehicle is used as a 'technical' – to carry a heavy machine gun or light anti-aircraft artillery piece. (ENDF)

Eritrean Expansion

Both sides exploited the lull in fighting to rearm and prepare for the next round. The ERDF continued intensive mobilisation and establishment of additional divisions to the degree where, by the summer of 1999, it operated a total of 18 fully developed divisions, organised as listed in Table 10.

In November 1998, and after plenty of pushing by Brigadier-General Hadgu, the first six MiG-29s were delivered to Eritrea. The aircraft arrived together with a significant number of contracted Ukrainian instructor pilots and technicians, a batch of 60 R-27 (ASCC code AA-7 Apex) medium range air-to-air missiles, and an unknown quantity of R-73 (ASCC code: AA-11 Archer) short range air-to-air missiles. They included one two-seat conversion trainer (serial number ERAF 501), and five single-seaters (serials ERAF 502-506). Only four pilots were available for them, all from the group originally trained in Italy and then in Ethiopia. They and Hadgu underwent a crash conversion course for MiG-29, in Russia, lasting only two weeks. Dejen Ande Hishel, one of the pilots involved, described the situation as follows:

'I went to Russia together with my childhood friend, Yonas Misghinna, Samuel Girmay, and Eyob Sealay. Our training was undertaken in great hurry and entirely inadequate. I was shocked when given a certificate from the Russians stating not only that I was a qualified pilot, but also qualified instructor pilot. Having only been taught the fundamentals, we never logged the sufficient number of flight hours, never trained formation flying or for combat, and thus we had no confidence in our abilities. I protested my premature graduation, but to no avail. My conclusion was that the Russians were more interested in meeting the goals of the higher-ups [in graduating students quickly; authors' note] than meeting our goals.'[115]

Once back in Eritrea, Dejen and his colleagues received further training from Hadgu, most of which was rather 'improvised' by nature. Eventually, they found out that their aircraft were old and frequently malfunctioning: the pilots thus began to mistrust not only their avionics, but their ejection seats in particular. Under the given circumstances, they were left without a choice but to conclude that they could do little else but attempt to deploy single aircraft to harass the fighter-bombers of the Ethiopian pilots with their R-27 missiles fired from maximum range. For easier orientation, a full list of MiG-29s confirmed as delivered to Eritrea in period 1998-2004, is provided in the Table 11.[116]

Table 10: ERDF Order of Battle, Summer 1999

Old Divisions	New Divisions
161 Division	Expanded into 161 Corps, including 16th, 26th, 36th and 46th Divisions
271 Division	Expanded into 271 Corps, including 17th 27th, 37th and 47th Division
381 Division	Expanded into 381 Corps, including 18th, 28th and 48th Divisions
471 Division	Expanded into 471 Corps, including 19th, 23rd, 29th, 39th and 49th Divisions
2000 Division	unclear

Table 11: ERAF MiG-29s, 1998-2004

Serial Number	Variant	Notes
ERAF 501	MiG-29UB	delivered in 1998; damaged during the war, required a major repair to return to service in 2001
ERAF 502	MiG-29	delivered in 1998; survived the Badme War
ERAF 503	MiG-29	delivered in 1998; shot down in February 1999
ERAF 504	MiG-29	delivered in 1998; survived the Badme War, grounded in 2001; overhauled in 2016 by team from Russia
ERAF 505	MiG-29	delivered in 1998; survived the war, grounded in 2001; overhauled in 2013 by team from Belarus; overhauled again in 2016 by team from Russia
ERAF 506	MiG-29	delivered in 1998; shot down in February 1999
ERAF 507	MiG-29	delivered in 2002; crashed in 2004
ERAF 508	MiG-29SMT	delivered in 2002; written off in a landing accident, in 2005
ERAF 509	MiG-29SMT	delivered in 2002; crashed in 2008
ERAF 510	MiG-29	dellvered in 2004; cannibalised for spares
ERAF 511	MiG-29	delivered in 2004; fate unknown
ERAF 512	MiG-29	delivered in 2004; overhauled in 2013 by team from Belarus

One of four MB.339s acquired by Eritrea as seen during pre-delivery trials, at Venegono airport, outside Varese. The aircraft had not yet received its full coat of camouflage colours at the time this photograph was taken. (Claudio Toselli Collection)

Another of the Eritrean Macchis as seen prior to delivery. Although apparently a 'light training jet', the MB.339 packed a very advanced nav/attack suite, and could deliver significant amounts of damage. (Claudio Toselli Collection)

'ERAF 505' was the fifth MiG-29 acquired by Eritrea. Notable is the application of the national marking in the form of a roundel – not only on the fin – but on the undersurface of the right wing too. Their primary armament consisted of R-27 and R-73 air-to-air missiles. (Photo by Dick Lohuis)

Organizing the Battlefield

Military preparations on the Ethiopian side were far more comprehensive. On the ground, the ENDF quickly reinforced its existing seven divisions, of which six were infantry and one a mechanized formation. Similarly, all of its specialised formations that were kept in strategic reserve were now expanded into divisions. These were organised into three corps, each of three divisions, equipped with a total of about 75 T-62s, a similar number of T-54/55s, 70 BRDM-1/2s, 20 BMP-1s and about 90 other armoured vehicles, and supported by nearly 500 heavy mortars and artillery pieces. Details about exact designations of units in question are unclear, while those about the distribution of this equipment remain scarce. It seems that all the available T-62s, BMP-1s, and self-propelled artillery pieces were concentrated in the only mechanized division, while each of the infantry divisions received a company of T-55s. The only detail certain is that the ENDF put in motion an extensive program of recruiting and training with the aim of enabling a massive counter-attack on Eritrea.[117]

On the contrary, much more is known about related activities of the EtAF. One of the most important changes related to the Ethiopian Air Force in the time immediately after the Eritrean attack on Badme was the fact that the government in Addis Ababa came to the decision to release Major-General Techane Mesfin from jail, and appoint him the Chief of Operations. This highly experienced officer, trained in the USA, quickly instilled a very aggressive spirit into the air force. Not only that the technicians of DAVEC had overhauled and returned to operations about a dozen additional combat and transport aircraft, but the EtAF worked extremely hard to reinstate its old structure of commands and to set up an integrated air defence system (IADS) covering northern and central Ethiopia. Related efforts were of particular importance because not only were the older MiG-21s and MiG-23BNs heavily dependent on ground support in order to be effectively operated: the same was the case with more modern fighter jets Ethiopia was about to acquire from Russia.

While Debre Zeit AB remained the main operational base (and the headquarters of the 1st Command EtAF), it became overcrowded by all the activity. Because Mekelle was, meanwhile, the hub of aerial operations against Eritrea, the local airport was extended and hardened, and the new 2nd Command EtAF established there (instead of the old 2nd Command based at Asmara). Each of these air bases became the centre of an IADS, each of which relied on equipment acquired from the former

During the early part of the warr, MiG-21bis forward deployed at Mekelle Airport were the only interceptors of the EtAF. This example was photographed while equipped with a 'full load' of air-to-air missiles, including two R-13Ms (AA-2C Atoll) and four R-60MKs (AA-8 Aphid). (EtAF via S.N.)

USSR in the 1970s and 1980s. The EtAF originally purchased a total of 7 S-75 Volga/Volkhov (ASCC code: SA-2 Guideline) surface-to-air (SAM) systems and 256 associated V-755 and V-759 missiles, and a further 10 S-125 Neva/Pechora (ASCC code: SA-3 Goa) SAM-systems and 366 associated V-601 missiles, in the period 1978-1985. However, because of other, more urgent issues, units equipped with these had never properly completed their training before the Soviet withdrawal in 1989. Indeed, while the complement of at least one of the SA-3 SAM-sites was captured by the EPLA in 1989-1990, most equipment still in Ethiopia fell into disrepair by 1998.[118]

Correspondingly, the government in Addis Ababa contracted an Israeli company to overhaul all the available SAMs and build-up an air defence system for the capital and for Mekelle. In turn,

the Israelis contracted a sizeable team of Ukrainian technicians and delivered a new, digital early warning radar of type D35D6, of Ukrainian origin, to Ethiopia.[119] This was combined with two Akkord 75/125A tactical management systems of Soviet/Russian origin to create two integrated air defence systems: one covering Mekelle and the battlefields of northern Tigray, and the other Debre Zeit and Addis Ababa. The home-base of the reinstated 4th Command and its MiG-23BNs – the more distant Bahir Dar AB – seems to not have been covered by such systems. The Ukrainian team completed most of its work by late 1998, and was subsequently withdrawn. The two IADS' were thus in place, but their personnel were still working up – meanwhile under Russian supervision – as of February 1999.[120]

Although already wearing the camouflage pattern applied during an overhaul at the DAVEC, this MiG-23BN was photographed while still marked with the old national insignia, replaced in December 1998. (Tom Cooper Collection)

Equipment of an Ethiopian S-125 Neva/Pechora SAM-site, as captured by Eritrean insurgents in 1991. Seven years later, both sides were deploying systems of this type. (Albert Grandolini Collection)

Foreign Instructors

The Eritrean invasion prompted many of the EtAF officers to return from exile and offer their service, while others were recalled from retirement. By September 1998, about 450 are known to have re-enlisted, including several returnees from Yemen, Kenya, and Uganda. A further seven pilots returned from their training in Romania. However, the war prompted the EtAF to re-assign all of its instructor pilots to combat units. Having a number of cadets in need of further training, and a mass of officers that required refresher training, or conversion courses to diverse combat aircraft and helicopters, but lacking their own instructor pilots, the government in Addis Ababa began searching for alternatives abroad.

Because they had already purchased old MiG-23BNs from Bulgaria (the aircraft in question were used as sources of spares for MiG-23BNs overhauled by the DAVEC), the Ethiopians were in contact with the Bulgarian company Okima – a subsidiary of the Quartz Company, owned by several prominent Bulgarian businessmen, and led by Malcho Malchev, a retired officer of the Bulgarian air force. Therefore, they requested Okima to provide a team of instructor pilots that would help convert a group of nine Ethiopian students that had just graduated their L-39-training, to MiG-21s. With Okima being slow to reply, a Russian company jumped in instead, providing five instructors. Very little is known about their activity in Ethiopia, except that one of their Ethiopian students crashed his MiG-21 in October 1998 during a training flight. After completing that part of their duty, the Russians were then contracted to convert a group of Ethiopians to L-39s. Another of their students, Captain Andagena Tadesse, crashed during that course, in November 1998, killing his Russian instructor, too.[121]

In the meantime, the Ethiopians continued negotiating with the Bulgarians, and Okima was contracted to provide basic and advanced jet training courses on L-39s to another group of nine Ethiopian pilots, who had just graduated from their basic training on the SF.260s. The Bulgarians arrived in Addis Ababa in late November 1998, and at first underwent their own conversion course on L-39s at Debre Zeit AB, which most of them had never flown before. However, intensive flying activity at that base prompted the Ethiopians to re-locate them to Gambela airfield, in north-western Ethiopia, close to the border with Sudan, where the EtAF basic flight school was, meanwhile, located. Despite immense problems caused by the heat, the Bulgarians helped the students – most of whom had some 100 hours in their logbooks, all flown on SF.260s – to complete a three-month course during which they soloed in navigation and basic fighter manoeuvring.[122]

By March 1999, the Bulgarian group and its students moved to Arba Minch, which offered more moderate weather, despite its position of 1,900 metres above the sea level. Using this airfield, the Bulgarians trained their Ethiopian students in air combat manoeuvring and weapons delivery. The training proceeded well until 20 April 1999 – the biggest religious feast in the Ethiopia – when two students were killed in two separate accidents – both of which were a result of unauthorised aerobatics at critically low altitudes. One Ethiopian clipped a lamp post with the wing of his L-39 about 17 kilometres north Arba Minch. The wreckage of his aircraft destroyed six houses and killed eight civilians. Similarly, the other crashed about 17 kilometres south of Arba Minch, causing unknown amount of damage and killing several civilians.

Subsequently, the Bulgarians and their students were sent back to Debre Zeit AB, where the seven Ethiopian survivors completed their basic weapons training on L-39s, from which they were converted straight to MiG-23BNs – this time under Russian supervision.[123]

Bulgarian instructors, and their Ethiopian students, in front of an EtAF L-39C. (Alexander Mladenov Collection)

One of the EtAF L-39Cs as seen airborne during a training sortie from Gambela airfield. (Aleksander Mladenov Collection)

Flanker Delivery

In the light of the provision of C-130 Hercules transports from the USA, Addis Ababa originally envisaged the purchase of second-hand combat aircraft – preferably General Dynamics/Lockheed-Martin F-16 Fighting Falcons – from the USA. However, these not only proved much too expensive, but also could never have been provided (and their crews trained) within the necessary period of time. Therefore, and because the Ethiopians knew that the Eritreans were in the process of buying MiG-29s, the EtAF opted for a batch of aircraft the Russians presented them as superior to that type: Sukhoi Su-27s (ASCC code: 'Flanker'). The corresponding contract was negotiated with Moscow in a matter of few days, in September 1998, and stipulated delivery of six Su-27SK interceptors, two Su-27UBK two-seat conversion trainers, 100 R-27ER/ET medium range air-to-air missiles (ASCC Code AA-10 Alamo), 100 R-73E short range air-to-air missiles, and conversion training for four Ethiopian pilots and a similar number of technicians and weapons specialists at Krasnodar, in Russia.[124]

The aircraft and support equipment were delivered to Dire Dawa AB on board chartered Ilyushin Il-76 and Antonov An-124 transports between 10 and 23 December 1998. Together with them arrived a group of about 300 Russian advisors, including lots of recently retired personnel of the Russian air force – amongst them several pilots that used to serve with the elite 237th Proscurov Air Technology Demonstration centre of the Guards, based at Kubinka AB, outside Moscow. Their nominal task was to keep the aircraft and their equipment operational for a period of six months.

Right from the start the Russian team had its hands full of work. As usual before and after, and whether converted to Su-27s in Russia, or in Ethiopia, the Russians provided only basic training in flying the type, but no training in air combat manoeuvring, none in weapons release, and even less so any tactical training. Therefore, once the aircraft were in Ethiopia, the Russian advisors had to help the Ethiopians complete their training and then develop their combat skills and suitable tactics. The first of the pilots converted to Su-27s in Ethiopia, in late 1998 and early 1999, was Lieutenant-Colonel Gebre Haile-Selassie, the future commander of the unit scheduled to operate the new type, No. 6 Squadron.[125]

However, the primary issue for everybody involved was the technical condition of the aircraft: it turned out that the Su-27s Moscow has sold to Addis Ababa were rather old. All were from early production batches and had already been in service with the Russian air force for about 15 years. Unsurprisingly, they were constantly suffering from poor reliability of their avionics, radio and hydraulic systems, and engines. Russian technicians thus had to work very hard to fix and tune their radars and other equipment. Simultaneously, the Russians had to train Ethiopian ground crews in how to maintain the aircraft – which was a process everybody knew would take most of 1999. All of these tasks were made even more complex by the fact that – in the urgency to get their Su-27s, but also in hope the conflict might be resolved through negotiations soon – the Ethiopians failed to buy all the support

equipment necessary to operate these complex jets and their armament, such as mobile testing systems.[126]

On 6 January 1999, towards the end of a flight demonstration in front of VIP-audience at Debre Zeit, the retired Russian Colonel Vyacheslav Myzin crashed one of the single-seaters. Reportedly, he was distracted for a second while underway at low altitude, fell into a spin due to the loss of speed, and was forced to eject while still inverted. Thanks to the excellent Zvezda K36 ejection seat, Myzin came away without any serious injuries. However, the Su-27SK was wrecked and a replacement aircraft had to be flown in from Russia. On the positive side, and while the Russians provided the replacement aircraft free of charge, this incident prompted the Ethiopians into the conclusion that a two-man crew is likely to decrease the heavy work-load in the cockpits of their Sukhois. Correspondingly, they placed an order for additional Su-27UBKs, at least nine of which were delivered by 2001.[127]

While the large Russian team continued helping the personnel of the No. 6 Squadron work up at Debre Zeit, the government in Addis Ababa contracted another – private – Russian company, Danubian, to provide instructor pilots to reinforce the Mi-24/35 crews of the 'Tiger Hunter' Squadron. Danubian is said to have provided four pilots that arrived in Ethiopia by December 1998 and are said to have served only a two-month tour of duty. Finally, sometimes during early 1999, Addis Ababa placed an order for four Su-25s in Moscow. Overall, through 1998-1999, the EtAF was thus organised and deployed as described in Table 12.[128]

One of the first four Su-27SKs delivered to Ethiopia was this example, serial number 1954. (ENTV)

The first Ethiopian Su-27UBK received the serial number 1901. Notable are multiple underwing hardpoints for R-27 and R-73 air-to-air missiles. (Pit Weinert Collection)

Table 12: EtAF Order of Battle, late 1999

Unit	Base	Aircraft Type	Tasks & Notes
No. ?? Tiger Hunter Squadron	Mekelle, Axum	Mi-24, Mi-35	25-28 helicopters
No. 3 Squadron	Bahir Dar, Mekelle	MiG-23BN	12-15 aircraft
No. 6 Squadron	Debre Zeit & Mekelle	Su-27SK & Su-27UBK	still working up, only 8 pilots partially ready for combat, supported by Russian personnel
No. 15 Squadron	Debre Zeit	An-12B, An-26, C-130B	5-6 An-12, 1 An-26, 2 C-130B
No. 20 Cheetah Squadron	Mekelle	MiG-21bis & MiG-21UM	15-20 aircraft
?? Flight	Mekelle	Su-25T & Su-25UBK	4 aircraft, delivered in late 1999
?? Squadron	Debre Zeit, Mekelle, Axum	Mi-8 & Mi-17	20-23 helicopters
Flight School	Debre Zeit, Gambela, Arba Minch	SF.260 & L-39	12-16 aircraft

Second Round

With months-long and intensive diplomatic activities resulting in no change of behaviour on the part of the government in Asmara, the government in Addis Ababa came to the conclusion that it would take a major counteroffensive to force the Eritreans out of all the areas they had meanwhile occupied, preferably before the next rainy season. Correspondingly, the ENDF put its units on alert, while all the schools and colleges in Mekelle, Axum and Adwa were closed by 28 January 1999.

Amongst the air force's units that were forward-deployed during the following days was No. 6 Squadron – meanwhile divided into two detachments: one based at Mekelle, with the task of providing top cover for ground troops fighting Eritreans, and the other at Debre Zeit, with the task of bolstering the air defences of the capital.[129] Considering the limited amount of spares and supporting equipment, this solution was far from ideal: throughout the following months, the team of Russian technicians continued maintaining Ethiopian Su-27s, all the time sorting out diverse problems with their avionics. Another major issue was the high altitude of most of the Ethiopian air bases: Debre Zeit and Mekelle were constructed at altitudes between 1600 and 1800 metres above sea level, and had runways with relatively rough surfaces. This not only significantly extended the take-off and landing runs of Su-27s (while increasing the wear on brake discs and the use of tyres), but also caused frequent engine failures due to the foreign object damage. Solutions found were, amongst others, to tow the aircraft to the start of the runway, and power up their engines only immediately before the start; to let the aircraft and their engines cool off for at least 45-55 minutes after landing and before the next take-off; and, to fly with less than maximum warload (theoretically consisting of up to 10 air-to-air missiles, full load of ammunition for internal 30mm cannon, and up to 8,000 litres of fuel in internal tanks). Overall, the Ethiopian Su-27 fleet was thus quite constrained in its operations, and frequently unable to stand quick reaction alerts.

However, it was soon to prove its worth. Reaching back upon experiences from the Ogaden War, and while still supported by Russian advisors, the pilots of No. 6 Squadron developed the tactics of baiting Eritrean interceptors with help of MiG-21s from No. 20 Squadron and the emerging IADS based in Mekelle. Accordingly, MiG-21s were to fly high over the battlefield, in order to attract the attention of the ERAF, with Su-27s orbiting at medium altitude, well behind them, and waiting for an Eritrean reaction. To decrease the workload of Ethiopian Su-27 pilots, the type was usually operated in mixed pairs, consisting of one single-seater and one two-seater, the crew of the latter usually including an Ethiopian pilot and a Russian advisor. However, aircraft manned by the Russians were strictly prohibited from even approaching the combat zone.[130]

With everything in place, the government in Addis Ababa decided to give Asmara four days to provide at least some response to numerous questions addressing its willingness to solve the dispute through negotiations. When there was no reply, the Ethiopians launched their counteroffensive. At 0400 hrs local time, on 2 February 1999, the ENDF's artillery opened an intensive barrage along the entire frontline from Cheraro in the west, via Shire, to Zalambessa in the centre. At dawn, Mi-24 and Mi-35 helicopters delivered a series of air strikes: they were to provide most of the CAS during the following weeks and months, primarily because of the mountainous nature of the battlefield, which hindered attacks by jet-propelled fighter bombers. By noon, the intensity of Ethiopian air strikes reached such proportions, that the ERDF was subsequently forced to limit its troop movements to the night.[131]

For four consecutive days, the entrenched Eritreans patiently endured Ethiopian air strikes and continuous artillery barrages, suffering losses all the time. Only the ERAF hit back in response: on 5 February 1999, two MB.339s bombed the fuel depot in Adigrat. Eritrean MiG-29s made their presence felt several times that day, too: their pilots – including Yonas Misghinna, Samuel Girmay, Dejen Ande Hishel and Eyob Sealay – fired multiple R-27Rs at EtAF's helicopters and MiG-23BNs from long range, but all of these missed. The Ethiopians reacted by directing at least one of the Su-27s towards the area in question, but the interceptor arrived much too late to catch any of the enemies. Instead, it nearly opened fire at a friendly Mi-8: the Ethiopian IADS in Mekelle was still working up, and frequently experiencing problems with its identification friend-or-foe (IFF) systems. The following night, the EtAF increased the pressure by deploying one of its An-12 as a makeshift-bomber: underway at high altitude, where it was outside the reach of Eritrean ground-based air defences, this unloaded a large number of general-purpose bombs through its rear-loading ramp, destroying an entire stretch of enemy fortifications in the process.[132]

Having its frontlines pulverised by days of Ethiopian air strikes and artillery barrages made the High Command of the ERDF nervous. Correspondingly, at dawn of 6 February 1999, it launched a full-scale attack on Ethiopian positions west, south and east of Badme, and in the Tsorona area. This appears to have been exactly what the High Command of the ENDF wanted: the Eritreans to exit the cover of their fortifications and attack, thus exposing themselves to the superior Ethiopian firepower. After a bitter battle that lasted most of the day, the ENDF successfully repelled all the assaults and then launched a counterattack that captured the Eritrean stronghold at Geza Gerlase, in the Tsorona area.[133] During follow-up operations, on 15 February 1999, the EtAF lost the Mi-35 flown by Majors Berihun Kidane (pilot) and Belhu Wasihun (weapons officer) to Eritrean ground-based air defences. Another helicopter from the same unit, a Mi-24, was written off under unknown circumstances on 24 February 1999.

In the air, the situation was meanwhile getting ever more tense, and it soon became clear that a decisive clash had to happen. After deploying one of their radar stations about five kilometres outside Adi Quala, some 50 kilometres north of Axum, and thus very close to the frontlines, the Eritreans attempted to set up an ambush of the Su-27s – only to get distracted by baiting MiG-21s, instead. A low-flying MiG-29 approached the Ethiopian bait just enough to fire a single R-27R from maximum range before its presence was detected by the other side. This time, the missile came close enough for the Ethiopian pilot to actually hear the detonation of the R-27's warhead, somewhere behind his aircraft. A pair of Ethiopian Su-27s fired two R-27ERs and two R-27ETs in return, but all of these missed their low-flying target. Seeking for ways to blind the ERAF, on the morning of 7 February 1999, the Ethiopians deployed their recently acquired 2S19 Msta-S self-propelled howitzers, with a range of 45 kilometres, to demolish the Eritrean radar station near Adi Quala – causing heavy losses to the ERAF personnel of this site. In retaliation, the ERAF's Macchis bombed Adigrat again, this time seriously injuring seven civilians. Once again, the Su-27s reacted by firing R-27s from long range, though this time at least one of the missiles failed to even launch. Only this incident prompted the EtAF to order the necessary testing equipment.[134]

During the following days, ERDF ground forces launched an all-out attempt to recover Geza Gerlase: however, all of their assaults were repelled with heavy loss. On the contrary, in the course of their counter-attacks, still supported by intensive air strikes of their Mi-24s, Mi-35s, and MiG-23BNs, the Ethiopians captured two further strongholds: Konin and Konito.

On 21 February 1999, the ERAF launched its second attempt to ambush one of the EtAF's Su-27s, this time by deploying two MiG-29 into a pincer attack. However, lacking the support of the destroyed radar station at Adi Quala, one of the MiGs flew straight into another Ethiopian ambush. After approaching at low altitude, it was detected while climbing to an altitude of 6,000 metres, in the direction of the baiting MiG-21s. Still 45 kilometres away, the pilot of the Su-27SK with serial number 1552 counterattacked by firing a single R-27ER: although his missile failed to hit its target, it forced the Eritrean MiG-29 to break and turn away. The Ethiopian followed in pursuit and fired a single R-27ET from a range of about 10 kilometres. This time, the missile proximity fused: the MiG was last seen while diving towards the ground, trailing a thick trace of smoke. Around this time, the other MiG-29 approached to about 20 kilometres from the Ethiopian interceptor, before climbing and firing a single R-27R. However, with the Sukhoi underway at a supersonic speed and an altitude of 6,000 metres, this attempt only resulted in another miss.[135]

One of only four Eritreans qualified to fly MiG-29s as of February 1990, Dejen Ande Hishel. (via S.N.)

One of about a dozen 2S19 Msta-S self-propelled howitzers acquired by the Ethiopians in late 1998. On 7 February 1999, they proved spectacularly successful in destroying a forward-deployed ERAF radar station outside Adi Quala. (Pit Weinert Collection)

According to unconfirmed reports, the ERAF MiG-29 damaged by an Ethiopian R-27ET on 21 February should have been this example, the MiG-29UB with serial number ERAF 501. The aircraft is known to have required complex repairs and an overhaul to be made flyable again, before this photograph was taken, in May 2001. (Photo by Dick Lohuis)

Although belonging to the second batch of Su-27SKs acquired by Ethiopia, this example – serial number 1967 – nicely illustrates the reduced warload the type had to carry during the Badme War because of high altitudes of local air bases. Visible is a single R-27ER (between the intakes), a pair of R-27ETs (centre underwing pylons) and a pair of R-73Es (outboard underwing pylons). (Pit Weinert Collection)

Left Hook at Badme: Operation Sunset

Satisfied with massive attrition imposed upon the ERDF, the Ethiopian High Command initiated Operation Sunset: a combined-arms operation during which its units were to punch through the heavily fortified Eritrean frontline and then conduct a high-speed manoeuvre deep into the enemy rear. By February 1999, the ENDF grew to 10 fully-deployed divisions: Operation Sunset was considered important enough for a full corps of three divisions to be kept in reserve only for this opportunity.[136]

In order to distract the Eritreans from the true intentions of the ENDF, the EtAF flew a high-profile air strike on Asseb airport, on 22 February 1999. Involving four MiG-23BNs this resulted in the local runway being cratered in multiple places. Additional air strikes, followed by a massive artillery barrage, then hit the Eritrean positions on the Tsorona front, thus feinting Ethiopian preparations for an attack on eastern or southern Eritrea.

At dawn of 23 February, the Ethiopians then launched their coup de main: starting from the old TPLF base in the Adi Ramets area, their three divisions punched through the Eritrean positions in the Biyakundi area and then advanced in the direction of Dukambiya before turning east and hitting the flank of the Division 2000, deployed in a waiting position north of Badme. Taken by surprise, the ERDF unit was almost completely destroyed in a horrific battle. The Ethiopians were thus free to continue their rapid advance all the way to Dukambiya, 20 kilometres south-east of Barentu. This action was decisive for the outcome of the entire war. Understanding that they were about to get cut off, commanders of the remaining Eritrean units deployed in the Badme area were left without a choice but to instantly abandon their positions, including nearly 100 kilometres of heavily fortified frontlines and most of their heavy arms. In a mad rush, their troops retreated north of the Mereb river, all the time heavily rocketed by EtAF helicopter gunships. Dozens of thousands of ERDF troops were killed, wounded or captured. With one blow, the ENDF thus restored control over virtually all of the territory that Eritrea had occupied for the preceding nine months.[137]

Ethiopian-operated M1977 self-propelled 122mm howitzer in action during Operation Sunset. (Pit Weinert Collection)

An Eritrean T-54/55 MBT, literally blown apart during Operation Sunset. (Pit Weinert Collection)

Eritrean T-54s in position at the Badme front in 1999. In addition to their coat of sand colour, notable are identification markings in form of large yellow circles, painted on turret sides. (ERDF)

Decisive Air Battles

The resulting crisis – probably the most severe the Eritreans experienced ever – had far reaching consequences. Amongst others, it caused a major disagreement between President Afewerki and the Chief-of-Staff ERDF, Major-General Abraha. After, once again, complaining about Afewerki's meddling into operational affairs, Abraha was dismissed and replaced by major-General Umar Hassan 'Tewil'. Furthermore, Afewerki ordered the ERAF into the skies, regardless of the cost. Therefore, on 25 February 1999, Yonas Misghinna was scrambled from Asmara AB with the intention of intercepting an Su-27 underway on a CAP north of Mekelle. Although making a detour in the direction of Badme before turning east and approaching at a very low altitude, his MiG-29 was detected and the Su-27SK with serial number 1954, flown by Lieutenant-Colonel Gebre-Selassie, was vectored to intercept. After finding his target, the Ethiopian fired two R-27ERs from a range of 27 kilometres: one of these has scored a direct hit, killing the Eritrean pilot and causing his aircraft to crash in flames.[138]

After this loss, it was more than clear that the Eritrean Air Force was an underdog in this conflict – even more so because the surviving pilots felt forced to fly combat sorties under impossible conditions. Dejen, one of only two surviving ERAF MiG-29 pilots as of late February 1999, recalled:

'I was sad and angry and filled with the wish to avenge Yonas' death. Normal procedure would have been to run an investigation and find out why was he shot down, in order to avoid similar mistakes in the future. In the meantime, we should have avoided repeating the pattern of the circumstances that led to the loss, which means flying over the same area,

altitude and speed of the downing. However, our government ignored all of this and ordered us into the sky again.'[139]

Nevertheless, on the next day, 26 February 1999, Samuel Girmay was scrambled in a MiG-29 from Asmara towards the south. There are at least three different versions of what happened as next. Along one, Girmay's MiG was detected while approaching Mendefera, still underway at a very low altitude. Lieutenant-Colonel Gebre-Selassie, this time on the Su-27SK with serial number 1958, was then vectored to intercept, and he shot down the Eritrean MiG with a single R-27ER fired from a range of well over 50 kilometres. According to the other, the presence of Girmay's MiG was first detected by the Ethiopian signals intelligence, when the Eritrean pilot made a radio call telling his ground control he had released one missile. According to the third, Gebre-Selassie fired two R-27ERs, both of which missed their target. The Eritrean was thus able to cut the range and fire at least one R-27R in return: however, Gebre-Selassie had meanwhile fired another missile – this time an infra-red homing R-27ET – and this hit home first, instantly killing the Eritrean pilot. Accordingly, after this high-speed engagement, the victorious Ethiopian was so short on fuel, on return to Mekelle he had barely 200 litres of fuel left in his tanks.[140]

In a matter of only two days, Ethiopian-operated Su-27s thus won the two decisive aerial victories against Eritrean-operated MiG-29s. Left with only two intact MiG-29 and only two pilots qualified to fly them, the ERAF never rose again to challenge the EtAF's aerial dominance. Worse yet: bitter complains by Dejen resulted in his arrest by the Eritrean military intelligence. He was held imprisoned in Asmara without charges, without verdict, or a day in court, for the next 15 years, until he managed to escape, in February 2014.[141]

Even years later, the Ethiopian Su-27SK with serial number 1958 still wore a kill marking commemorating the 'kill' it scored on 26 February 1999. This was applied in the form of a red star, on either side of the front fuselage, right behind the serial. (Pit Weinert Collection)

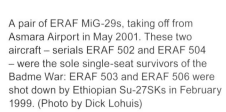

A pair of ERAF MiG-29s, taking off from Asmara Airport in May 2001. These two aircraft – serials ERAF 502 and ERAF 504 – were the sole single-seat survivors of the Badme War: ERAF 503 and ERAF 506 were shot down by Ethiopian Su-27SKs in February 1999. (Photo by Dick Lohuis)

Operation Westwind

Despite their overwhelming success, the Ethiopians knew all too well that the Eritreans were extremely unlikely to give up. On the contrary, through the mass of reports about the flight of many Eritreans who opposed forced recruitment (often at gunpoint) into southern Sudan, they correctly assessed that the ERDF was undertaking everything possible to recover the strength of its units within the shortest period of time, and to reinforce and reorganise its frontlines. Using remaining reserves, it established a sub-command of its Centre Front under the direct command of Major-General Umar Hassan 'Tewil'. Deploying and distributing reinforcements became extremely problematic, because – free from the threat of Eritrean MiG-29s – Ethiopian Mi-24s, Mi-35s, MiG-21s and MiG-23BNs were constantly attacking any troop concentrations they were able to find, but also Eritrean logistic links and the water supply system. Furthermore, An-12s continued their nocturnal bombing sorties. This bought enough time for the ENDF to construct a heavily fortified defence line from Biyakundi in the West to the Mereb River in the north and then to Dukambiya and Shambuko in the centre.

With a major Eritrean counter-offensive failing to materialise, the Ethiopians decided to resume their attacks. Correspondingly, on 15 March 1999 they launched Operation Westwind, in the central sector. This saw two divisions of the ENDF advancing from Rama in the direction of Tsorona in the west, and from Adigrat in the direction of Zalambessa, provoking a four-day clash known to the Eritreans as the 'Battle of Igri-Mekel'. Both sides subsequently claimed a victory: Asmara reported its forces to have killed 10,000 Ethiopians, while Addis Ababa claimed 9,000 killed Eritreans. Furthermore, the crew of the EtAF Mi-35 with serial number 2108 was forced to land behind Eritrean positions due to a problem with its hydraulics system, on 18 March 1999. All three crewmembers and eight militiamen it transported were captured by the Eritreans, who then deployed their former EtAF technicians working for the ERAF to repair the helicopter. This Mi-35 was subsequently flown to Asmara: however, as far as is known, it was never deployed in combat.[142]

Eventually, Operation Westwind did not result in the success expected by the Ethiopians. However, it did prompt the leadership in Asmara into several important decisions. Amongst others, it

Satisfied troops inside one of the Eritrean positions on the Tsorna front in early 1999. (Photo by Dan Connell)

grounded its air force, and instead concentrated on the ground battle only, as commented by Dejen:

'After the Battle of Igri-Mekel, a decision was taken which I could not comprehend. I was told that the fighter jets are grounded and would not participate in fighting any more. To me, this did not make sense. The battlefield was only 80-90 kilometres distance from Asmara, and we could still fly relatively safe sorties, strike and come back.'[143]

Landscape of the Tsorona front, with several bodies of Ethiopian troops left behind after one of many local attacks. (Photo by Dan Connell)

A pair of Ethiopian T-54/55 MBTs, knocked out by Eritrean defences during Operation Westwind in March 1999. (ERDF)

Battle of Attrition

The much-expected Eritrean counteroffensive came only two weeks later, but the related reporting from Asmara only indicated how deep the Ethiopians had advanced into Eritrea. On 29 March 1999, the Eritrean media announced a 'successful counteroffensive on the front near Mereb River', in the course of which the ERDF forces claimed to have killed or captured 3,400 Ethiopian troops, captured one and destroyed eight tanks, and one ZU-23 anti-aircraft cannon. In reality, the ENDF was well-entrenched in its new position and thus repelled all the counter-attacks. Furthermore, on 16 April 1999, four MiG-23BN delivered a spectacular air strike on the Sawa Military Training Camp, in western Eritrea, causing significant damage. As one of the most important military bases of the ERDF – including a small airfield – this crucial installation was reportedly protected by one of two 2K12 Kub (ASCC code: SA-6 Gainful) SAM-systems operated by the Eritreans. Nevertheless, this was taken by surprise and failed to open fire in return. Similarly, the second ERDF counteroffensive on the Mereb River frontline, undertaken by four brigades on 24 May 1999, was repelled, with over 400 Eritreans killed and about 1,500 wounded. The EtAF is known to have lost one of its Mi-35s on that date. However, related details remain evasive.[144]

Rushing new troops to the front, the Eritreans launched their third attack between 9 and 13 June 1999, initially scoring an apparent success. However, the ENDF only let them get through its frontlines before closing the frontline behind the advancing Eritreans and then destroying them. The EtAF is known to have lost one of its helicopters during this battle, on 11 June, when the Mi-35 flown by Captains Zenebe Mideksa (pilot) and Eshetu Bekele (weapons officer) was shot down by ground fire, somewhere in the Dukambiya area.[145]

Despite all the setbacks, the ERDF continued trying. Between 25 and 29 June 1999, it launched two additional counter-offensives over the Mereb River. Continuously bombed and rocketed by the EtAF, helicopter gunships and fighter-bombers of which attacked any enemy troop concentration they could find, and hit by massive Ethiopian artillery barrages, the Eritreans were repulsed again – prompting Addis Ababa into claiming to have inflicted over 20,000 casualties upon the enemy in that month alone. Regardless of whether such claims by Addis Ababa can be trusted or not, there is little doubt that the result of the fighting between February and June 1999 was an outright disaster for the ERDF. Its heavy losses, followed by the rainy season, once again stopped all fighting for the next few months.

A still from a video showing an EtAF pilot about to embark his MiG-23BN for the next combat sortie in 1999. The aircraft was loaded with four RBK-250 CBUs. (ENTV)

Eritrean Problems

Although its troops were meanwhile firmly in control of the Badme region and most other disputed areas, the government in Addis Ababa was in no position to dictate conditions. On the contrary: because of the massive material and human cost of the war it was also keen to end fighting through negotiations. However, concerned about its own survival in the case the extent of its defeat would become known to the Eritrean public, the government in Asmara was anxious to cover up the entire affair through making martial announcements about victories, and supposed Ethiopian threats to destroy the entirety of Eritrea, while refusing to make binding concessions on the diplomatic plan. Indeed, the government of President Afewerki then launched a diplomatic offensive with the aim of presenting itself as a victim of Ethiopian aggression, thus buying the time necessary to reorganise and re-equip its battered military. This resulted in nearly six months of often intensive negotiations

mediated by the OAU and Algeria, and various other foreign powers too.

While no details are available about what the ERDF did in order to rebuild its ground forces in 1999, it is quite certain that it experienced extreme difficulties – foremost because it found next to no sources ready to deliver armament. A good example of related problems is what happened to the ERAF during the year 1999. Supported by his team of ex-EtAF personnel and several contracted Ukrainians, Brigadier-General Hadgu spent most of his time training the second group of Eritrean pilots to fly MiG-29s. His efforts were hampered by the fact that only two aircraft were left in operational condition, and that the stock of ammunition and spares for them were meanwhile critically low. The government in Asmara did attempt to obtain additional aircraft, spares and armament, and corresponding requests were forwarded to Moscow. Indeed, the government of Russia answered positively. However, the six MiG-29s from this order were delivered to Asmara only after the Badme War. In similar fashion, while agreeing to sell Su-27s, Russia began delivering these only in 2003, and then provided only two aircraft – one single- and one two-seater – simply because Asmara failed to pay for more. The principal reason for the Russian reluctance was that Moscow was already involved neck-deep in Ethiopia, and had an order for four Sukhoi Su-25s and a batch of Mi-17 helicopters from Addis Ababa on its books: the Kremlin was not keen to start providing armament to both parties at the same time.

For similar reasons, but also the combination of international pressure and sanctions, Eritrean negotiations for the acquisition of aircraft from the governments of Georgia, Italy, Finland, Moldavia, and Ukraine all remained fruitless. Italy and Finland turned down all the requests for spare parts required for Redigos and Macchis. The ERAF was thus forced to ground all aircraft of these two types and stop conducting training of novice pilots. Overall, reports about deliveries of six MiG-21s, eight Su-25s, and additional MiG-29s from late 1999 and early 2000, all proved unrealistic: for all practical purposes Asmara not only failed to obtain new armament, but even to properly re-stock its depleted stocks of ammunition.[146]

On the Ethiopian side of the frontlines, the year 1999 was foremost characterised by the arrival of further reinforcements – most of which were direct results of massive investment into intensive training and expansion of the ENDF, launched in June of the previous year. Amongst others, the army acquired 18 WAC-021 towed 155mm artillery pieces and 25 Type-63 towed multiple rocket launchers from China, and over 100 additional D-30 howitzers from diverse sources. Through maintenance and overhaul of heavy weapons de-facto abandoned in May 1991, the Ethiopians increased the number of available T-54 and T-55 MBTs to about 450, in turn expanding their mechanised forces by a magnitude. No less than four mechanised divisions – the 4th, 6th, 7th and 8th – were operational by early 2000, while the number of infantry divisions was increased to 22.

The intensive training of the EtAF also began to pay dividends. By October 1999, the number of available MiG-21bis' and MiG-23BNs each grew to about 20. A month later, enough ground crews had completed their conversion courses on Su-27s for the No. 6 Squadron to be declared fully operational. By then this unit was reinforced to at least 12 aircraft through the addition of

The Su-27UBK serial number 1907 belonged to the second batch of such aircraft ordered by Ethiopia in early 1999. (EtAF via S.N.)

a few Su-27UBKs from the second batch ordered early that year. Still commanded by Lieutenant-Colonel Gebru, the squadron meanwhile included a mix of four pilots trained in Russia and four trained in Ethiopia. Unfortunately, it suffered an early loss on 8 December 1999, when one of the younger pilots trained in Russia, Lieutenant Abayneh, was killed during a training sortie.[147]

Late in December 1999, the four Sukhoi Su-25 that the Ethiopians ordered from Russia were delivered on board a chartered transport aircraft to Debre Zeit. All were second-hand aircraft, taken from the stocks of the Russian air force: they included two Su-25UB two-seat conversion trainers with combat capability, and two Su-25Ts, which was a reasonably advanced variant equipped for deployment of precision guided ammunition. The two Su-25Ts were operated by a separate flight and flown by experienced MiG-23BN pilots. They went into action starting in January 2000 and were primarily deployed to strike high-value targets – such as command posts and supply depots – by night. Although flying some of most dangerous sorties of the war, and despite multiple claims of destruction by Eritrean ground defences (for example: on 15 May 2000), not one was ever shot down.

Lacking heavy weapons and mobility, the ERDF was forced to improvise during the Badme War. In this case, the Eritreans installed a D-30 howitzer atop the chassis of a T-54/55 MBT. (ERDF)

Sporting the new national insignia, introduced in December 1998, and a chaff and flare dispenser installed low on the rear fuselage, this EtAF MiG-23BN was photographed while returning from a sortie, at Bahir Dar AB. The national insignia was subsequently moved to the centre of the fin. (S. N. Collection)

The Final Act

On 12 May 2000, Ethiopia launched its final offensive of this war, this time on the Central Front. The initial objective of this operation was to breach the Eritrean positions before Shambuko and Shelalo, and capture Tokombia, with the aim of forcing the ERDF to re-deploy some of its units from the Zalambessa area, and thus facilitate a subsequent offensive in this area – or, alternatively, to compel Eritrea to negotiate a cessation of hostilities.[148]

This time, the Ethiopians subjected Eritrean positions to two days of air strikes and artillery barrages before actually lunching their assault on the morning of 14 May. By then, the Eritreans collapsed quickly: within the following 24 hours, the Ethiopians seized Tokombia, then Bishuka, Mailem and Molki. The Eritreans counterattacked near Shambuko and Bimbina, but were repelled, and the Ethiopians entered Barentu on 18 May. While supporting this operation, the EtAF lost another Mi-24, which crashed in the Gefersa area, killing its crew of two Ethiopians, and a Russian advisor. Another helicopter gunship was damaged, but its crew managed to land safely behind Ethiopian lines. There were rumours that in the course of this operation the Ethiopian Su-27s shot down another Eritrean MiG-29, but no confirmation was ever provided for this and no ERAF pilot with the rank and name 'Major Workneh' is known to have existed. Most likely, such reports were caused by sighting of a lone Eritrean MiG-29 in the skies west of Asmara during an air raid by two MiG-23BNs

against the port of Massawa. As often by the time, Ethiopian fighter-bombers were escorted by a pair of Su-27s: their pilots detected the Eritrean MiG, but did not engage because of standing order to make sure the MiG-23BNs would return safely to their base.

As well as bombing Massawa, the EtAF also launched a spectacular attack by four MiG-23BNs on the Eritrean SA-6 SAM-site outside Mendefera, on 20 May 2000. Taken by surprise, the Eritrean unit was subjected to almost simultaneous attack from multiple directions – during which a mix of parachute-retarded CBUs and general-purpose bombs was released – and almost completely destroyed. Asmara reacted with reports of having shot down four MiG-23BNs on 24 May alone, and two others in an attack on Adi Deyib, a day later. However, the Eritrean air defences and front lines were in the process of collapsing: the Ethiopians actually ranged wide and far over the battlefield, without encountering any serious resistance and not one MiG-23BN is known to have been lost in combat during the entire Badme War.[149]

Once through the Eritrean frontlines, the ENDF immediately exploited the opportunity to apply what its former TPFL-commanders knew the best: manoeuvring warfare. Correspondingly, the 15th Division was unleashed into a headlong advance from Barentu along the road to Tesseney. Underway in the western direction, this division overran multiple Eritrean rear

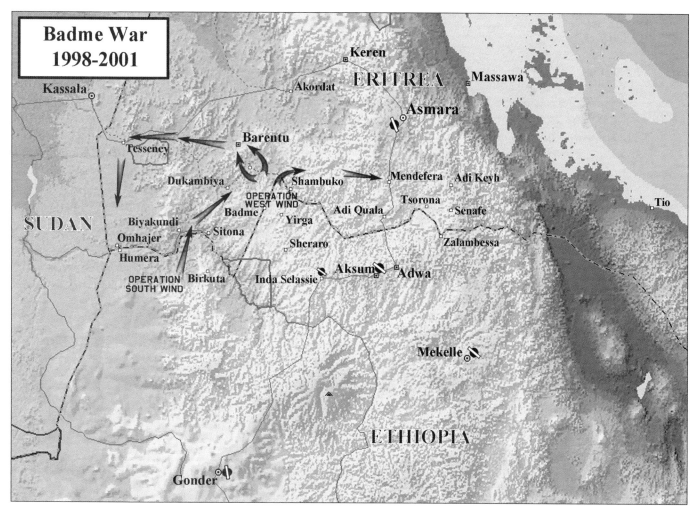

Map 6 The Badme War, with a reconstruction of the most-important manoeuvres by the ENDF during Operations South Wind and West Wind (in 2000). (Map by Tom Cooper)

65

bases before encountering serious resistance at Haykota, on 27 May, and then taking Tesseney a day later. Fresh Eritrean forces arriving from the Sawa base came much too late to prevent the fall of the town, but their counterattack on 4 June did force the 15th Division to withdraw south of the Setit River on 4 June 2000. Instead of falling back, the Ethiopians then punched through at Um Hajger, reinforced the 15th with three other divisions and re-launched their advance towards north, re-capturing Guluj on 12 June, and Tesseney and Alighidir two days later.[150]

Meanwhile, two Ethiopian MiG-23BNs had bombed the newly constructed power plant near Hirgigo, ten kilometres outside Massawa, on 28 May 2000.[151] Only a day later, two MiG-23BNs – each carrying four FAB-500M-62 general-purpose bombs – raided Asmara airport for the last time. After approaching their target at a very low altitude along meticulously planned routes – because they expected fierce resistance – the Ethiopians took the Eritreans by surprise, cratered the runway and bombed out one of the spare parts depots, before turning around to strafe with cannon fire. Amongst others, they managed to hit the control tower and one of the MB.339s parked inside a hangar (the aircraft in question was non-operational and had been used as a source of spares for some time). The two fighter-bombers were out of sight before even a single Eritrean managed to return their fire. A single MiG-29 was scrambled minutes after the Ethiopians departed, but it was too late to mount a successful intercept. Furthermore, the MiG-23BNs were escorted by a pair of Su-27s.

Finally finding an opportune moment, and following a tremendous artillery barrage, on 28 May 2000 the Ethiopians overran the Eritreans in Zalambessa, and – further increasing the pressure on an obviously battered enemy – launched an advance along the road from Bure to Asseb, the port of which was bombed by two MiG-23BNs on 2 June 2000. By this point in the war, the ENDF could have easily captured this city – which was exactly what its commanders (and most of the Ethiopian political opposition) demanded. However, the government in Addis Ababa turned down all such requests out of concern for being accused of an 'invasion'. Correspondingly, this advance was stopped about 37 kilometres (23 miles) outside the southern Eritrean port.

The End of the Badme War

Satisfied with the achievements of its military, and in firm control of nearly a third of Eritrea, Addis Ababa then stopped further offensive operations. On 18 June, even Asmara accepted the Ethiopian offer for a comprehensive peace agreement, combined with binding arbitration of their disputes. Through the mediation of the UN, a 25-kilometre-wide, 'Temporary Security Zone' was established within Eritrea, patrolled by the United Nations Mission in Ethiopia and Eritrea, including troops from more than 60 countries. A corresponding peace agreement was signed by both governments on 12 December 2000. The ruling of the Permanent Court of Arbitration in The Hague from April 2002, awarded some territory to each side: Badme went to Eritrea, while diverse parts of southern Eritrea were awarded to Ethiopia. Following initial disagreements, and despite immense significant pressure from within, both governments in Addis Ababa and Asmara eventually accepted this ruling.[152]

On 21 December 2005, a commission at the Permanent Court of Arbitration in The Hague ruled that Eritrea broke international law when it attacked Ethiopia in 1998, triggering the war, and declared the country liable to pay for the damage the conflict has caused. Both countries reacted by remobilising their troops along the border, and Eritrea banned flights of UN-operated helicopters. However, no new war erupted.[153]

With both sides accusing each other of supporting dissidents and armed opposition groups, tensions between Ethiopia and Eritrea remain high today. Nevertheless, a new armed conflict of the scope of the Badme War from 1998-2001 is relatively unlikely. Not only that both countries ended that war completely exhausted, Eritrea has never managed to fully recover its earlier military power, while the UN has confirmed its claim on the Badme area. On the other hand, Ethiopia emerged from the Badme War not only as victorious, and with its military reputation fully restored, but as an outright powerhouse in this part of Africa. Foremost, the situation in Somalia has heated up again ever since, drawing away most of the attention of Addis Ababa, while Asmara has no incentive to re-start the fighting. Correspondingly, and although not entirely solved, the conflict between Ethiopia and Eritrea is likely to remain 'on hold' for a number of years longer.

BIBLIOGRAPHY

Africa Watch Report, Evil Days: 30 years of War and Famine in Ethiopia, September 1991, via www.hrw.org.

Amdemichael, Haile Araya, 'East African Crisis Response: Shaping Ethiopian peace force for better participation in future peace operations', (Thesis, Naval Postgraduate School, Monterey, California, 2006).

Ayele, Fantahun, *The Ethiopian Army: From Victory to Collapse, 1977-1991*, (Northwestern University Press: Evanston, Illinois, 2014, ISBN 978-0-8101-3011-1).

Ayele, Fantahun, 'Operation Flame and the Destruction of the 3rd Division', in *The Ethiopian Journal of Social Sciences* Volume 1, Number 1, May 2015.

Berhe, Aregawi, 'A Political History of the Tigray People's Liberation Front (1975-1991): Revolt, Ideology and Mobilisation in Ethiopia', (Thesis, 2008, Vrije Universiteit).

Clapham, Christopher, *African Guerrillas: Eritrea/Tigray/Sudan/Somalia/Uganda/Rwanda/Congo-Zaire/Liberia/Sierra Leone*, (Oxford: James Currey Ltd, 1998, ISBN 0-85255-815-5).

Clapham, Christopher, 'The Ethiopian Coup d'Etat of December 1960', in *The Journal of Modern African Studies* Vol. 6, No. 4 (December 1968), pp.495-507.

Connell, Dan, *Against all odds: A Chronicle of the Eritrean Revolution*, (Asmara: The Red Sea Press Inc., 1997, ISBN 0-56902-046-9).

Connell, Dan, *Taking on the Superpowers: Collected Articles on the Eritrean Revolution (1976-1982), Vol.1*, (Trenton: The Red Sea Press Inc., 2003, ISBN 1-56902-188-0).

Connell, Dan, *Building a new nation; Collected articles on the Eritrean Revolution (1983-2002), Vol.2*, (Trenton: The Red Sea Press Inc., 2004, ISBN 1-56902-198-8).

Cooper, T., Weinert, P., with Hinz, F., and Lepko, M., *African MiGs: MiGs and Sukhois in Service in Sub-Saharan Africa, Volume 1, Angola to Ivory Coast* (Houston: Harpia Publishing, 2010 ISBN 978-0-9825539-5-4).

Cooper, T., *Wings over Ogaden: The Ethiopian-Somali War, 1978-79, Africa@War 18* (Sollhull: Helion & Company Ltd and Pinetown, 30° South Publishers (Pty) Ltd., 2015, ISBN 978-1909982-38-3).

Director of Central Intelligence Agency, *The Status of Cuban Military Forces in Ethiopia*, Interagency Intelligence Memorandum, 2 September 1981.

Eritrea Profile, 'North Eastern Sahel Front: From birth to demise Part I' in *Eritrea Profile*, Vol. 21 No 5, 19 March 2014.

Fontrier, Marc, *La chute de la junte militaire éthiopienne, 1987-1991*, (Paris: L'Harmattan, 1999, 2007 ISBN 978-2-84586-736-9).

Feleke, Zenebe, *It Happened Like That (Naber, in Amharic)*, (printed privately, 2004), no ISBN; author was imprisoned from 1991 until 1998 and dedicated his publication to a person that helped him smuggle the original of this manuscript out of Ethiopia for publishing

Flintham, V., *Air Wars and Aircraft: A Detailed Record of Air Combat, 1945 to the Present* (London: Arms and Armour Press, 1989 ISBN 0-8536-779-X).

Hughes, Howard, *Eine Volksarmee besonderer Art – der Militärkomplex in Eritrea*, December 2004.

Gorgu, Col Girma, *Let History Speak for Itself (Yinager Tariku, in Amharic)*, (Miazia: Birhan and Selam Printing Press, 2003).

HRW, 'Mengistu has Decided to Burn Us like Wood: Bombing of Civilians and Civilian Targets by the Air Force', *Human Rights Watch*, 24 July 1990.

Jackson, P., 'Death of an Air Force', *AirForces Monthly*, June 1993.

Kotlobovskiy, A. B., *MiG-21 in Local Conflicts (MiG-21 v Lokalnih Konfliktah, in Russian)*, (Kiev: ArchivPress, 1997).

Lefebvre, Jeffrey A., *Arms for the Horn: U.S. Security Policy in Ethiopia and Somalia, 1953-1991*, (Pittsburgh: University of Pittsburgh Press, 1992, ISBN 978-0822985334).

'Eritreans Attack Polish Ship', *Los Angeles Times*, 8 January, 1990.

Marcus, Harold G., *A History of Ethiopia* (Updated Edition), (Berkeley: University of California Press, 1994, ISBN 0-520-22479-5).

Markakis, John, *Ethiopia: The Last Two Frontiers* (Oxford, James Currey, 2011, ISBN 978-1847010339).

May, Clifford D., *Ethiopian Train Falls off Bridge; 392 are killed*, New York Times, 15 July 1985.

Melake, Tekeste, 'The Battle of Shire – February 1989; a turning point in the protracted War in Ethiopia', ethiopianreview.com.

Million Eyob, 'The Anti-colonial Political and Military Struggle Part VII and VIII', www.shabait.com (22 March 2013).

Möller, Harald, *DDR und Äthiopien, Unterstützung für ein Militärregime (1977-1989)*, (Berlin: Verlag Dr. Hans-Joachim Köster, 2003, ISBN 3-89574-492-1).

Mulugeta Gebrehiwot Berhe, 'The Ethiopian post-transition security sector reform experience: building a national army from a revolutionary democratic army', *African Security Review*, Volume 26, 18 April 2017.

National Photographic Interpretation Center, Imagery analysis report, 'Cuban Combat Forces in Ethiopia(S)', January 1981.

Nkaisserry, Brig Joseph K., *The Ogaden War: An Analysis of its Causes and its Impact on Regional Peace on the Horn of Africa* (Carlisle Barracks: Strategic Research Project, US Army War College, 1997).

Pateman, Roy, *Eritrea: Even the stones are burning*, (Asmara, The Red Sea Press Inc, 1998, ISBN 1-56902-057-4).

Pool, David, *From Guerrillas to Government: The Eritrean People's Liberation Front* (Oxford: James Currey, 2001, ISBN 978-0-8255-853-9).

Prunier, Gérard, *L'Éthiopie contemporaine*, (Paris, Karthala, 2007, ISBN 978-2-84586-736-9).

Sarin., Gen O., Dvoretsky, Col L., *Alien Wars: The Soviet Union's Aggressions Against the World, 1919 to 1989* (Novato: Presidio Press, 1996).

Scuttts, J., *Northrop F-5/F-20* (Osceola: Motorbooks International, 1986, ISBN 0-7110-1576-7).

Shifaw, Dawit, *The Diary of Terror: Ethiopia 1974 to 1991*, (Trafford Publishing, 2012, ISBN 978-1-4669-4524-1).

Shinn David H. et al, *Historical Dictionary of Ethiopia*, (Scarecrow Press, 2013, ISBN 978-0810871946).

Tareke, Gebru, *Ethiopia, Power & Protest, Peasants Revolts in the Twentieth Century* (Asmara: The Red Sea Press Inc. 1996, ISBN 1-56902-019-1).

Tareke, Gebru, *The Ethiopian Revolution: War in the Horn of Africa* (Yale University Press, 2009, ISBN 978-0-300-14163-4).

Tesfai, Alemseged, *Two Weeks in the Trenches: Reminiscences of Childhood and War in Eritrea* (Asmara: The Red Sea Press Inc, 2003, ISBN 978-1569021699).

Weldemichael, Awet T., 'The Eritrean Long March: The Strategic Withdrawal of the Eritrean People's Liberation Front (EPLF), 1978-1979', *The Journal of Military History*, 73 (October 2009).

Young, John, 'The Tigray and Eritrean People's Liberation Fronts: A History of Tensions and Pragmatism', *The Journal of Modern African Studies*, 34, I, 1996.

NOTES

1 'Rebels Claim they downed Ethiopian Fighter Jet', AP, 23 April 1984. As described in Volume 18 of Africa@War, Petros was originally trained in Ethiopia and then the USA, and used to fly F-5A/Es early during his career. He was with the first group of Ethiopian pilots that underwent a conversion course on MiG-23s in the USSR.

2 'Evil Days: 30 Years of War and Famine in Ethiopia', An Africa Watch Report, September 1991, pp.194-199.

3 Ayele 2014, p.158; Tareke 2009; p.109; Aregawi Berhe, pp.173 & 316 & Tekeste Melake.

4 Fontrier, pp.153-154.

5 'Evil Days: 30 Years of War and Famine in Ethiopia', pp.320-321; Fontrier, pp.156-158 & Ayele 2014, p.49.

6 Ayele 2014, pp.58-59; 'Ethiopia: The Mengistu Regime and Its Relations With Moscow', CIA, ALA 84-10084X, August 1984 & 'Hind Deployment, Cubcub Airfield, Ethiopia', NPIC/PEG (05/82), Z-10684/82, CIA, FOIA Electronic Reading Room (henceforth 'CIA/FOIA/ERR'). In northern Ethiopia of the mid-1980s, the army's Mi-24s and Mi-35s maintained regular detachments at a number of forward operating locations, including Agordat, Cubcub, Keren, and Gode.

7 'Ethiopia: Political and Security Impact of the Drought', CIA, Office of African and Latin American Analysis, ALA 85-10039, April 1985, CIA/FOIA/ERR, p.4 & 'Evil Days: 30 Years of War and Famine in Ethiopia', An Africa Watch Report, September 1991, pp.187-188. Amongst others, the latter report cited:
    'In 1989, the sale of relief food by the army and militia in Eritrea had reached such a scale that a brisk trade was being conducted across the battle lines into Tigray, where it was contributing a significant amount of the diet of people and keeping food prices low.'

8 Ethiopia: Political and Security Impact of the Drought', CIA, Office of African and Latin American Analysis, ALA 85-10039, April 1985, CIA/FOIA/ERR, p.4.

9 'Ethiopia: The Mengistu Regime and Its Relations With Moscow', CIA, ALA 84-10084X, August 1984, CIA/FOIA/ER & Joanne Omang, 'Ex-Official Says Ethiopia Mired in "No-Win" War', Washington Post, 9 February 1987. Despite Ethiopian complaints, it cannot be denied that the Soviets were providing their arms under quite favourable conditions. Usually, Ethiopia was able to purchase most heavy equipment at half its list price, with repayment over 10 years, at only two percent annual interest.

10 Ayele 2014, pp.58-59 & 72; Fontrier, p.148.

11 'Fishbed Aircraft Delivery, Aseb Port Facilities, Ethiopia', NPIC/PEG (9/83), Z-14987/83, CIA/FOIA/ERR. The report in question cited the delivery of nine 'Fishbed fuselage shipping containers' – i.e. nine MiG-21s – on board the Soviet Nikolay Zhukhov-class merchant ship, in summer 1983. A cross-examination of known serial numbers and recollections of former EtAF personnel has shown that Ethiopia imported more than 100 MiG-21bis and about 50 MiG-23BNs between 1977 and 1991.

12 While the Soviet and Russian press frequently described these commands as 'regiments', and the Western press as 'wings', the Ethiopians called them 'ayer mid'b', which literally means 'command'.

13 'Ethiopia: The Impact of Soviet Military Assistance', CIA, ALA 83-10005, January 1983, CIA/FOIA/ERR.

14 Cooper et al, African MiGs, Volume 1, pp.159-169; Taylor, World's Air Forces, p.54. Despite multiple reports about the acquisition of licence-manufactured Alouette IIIs in the form of HAL Cheetak and IAR.316Bs, Ethiopia never bought any of these. Instead, the 14th Squadron EtAF continued flying three SA.316Bs acquired from France in the early 1970s.

15 'Ethiopia: The Mengistu Regime and Its Relations With Moscow', CIA, ALA 84-10084X, August 1984, CIA/FOIA/ERR.

16 'Evil Days: 30 Years of War and Famine in Ethiopia', pp.203-204.

17 'Mengistu has Decided to Burn Us like Wood', An Africa Watch Report, p.14.

18 Ayele 2014, p.159; Tareke 2009, p.263; Tekeste Melake &, 'Mengistu has Decided to Burn Us like Wood', p.14.

19 Operation Adwa was named after the famous victory of Emperor Menelik against the Italians in 1898.

20 Ayele 2014, p.160; Tareke 2009; pp.263-264 & Dawit Shifaw, p.155.

21 'Mengistu has Decided to Burn Us like Wood', pp.21-22; 'Evil Days: 30 Years of War and Famine in Ethiopia', pp.253-254 & Flintham, p.147. According to the first two reports, the TPLF initially reported about 360 killed and 500 buildings destroyed. Later on, it published estimates of up to 1,300 fatalities, while locals estimated the number of killed at between 1,800 and 2,000.

22 Tareke 2009, p.267. Ethiopian airmen were not the only ones to commit atrocities against civilians. The army burned down most of the villages it captured during its initial advance into Tigray and summarily executed hundreds, if not thousands of people suspected of collaborating with the insurgents.

23 'Mengistu has Decided to Burn Us like Wood', p.9.

24 Ayele 2014, pp.162-163 & Tareke 2009, pp.270-271.

25 Ayele 2014, p.163 & Tareke 2009, pp.271.

26 Tareke 2009, p.272 & TPLF Communiqué 6/89.

27 Ayele 2014, pp.164-166; Tareke 2009, pp.272-275; TPLF Military Communiqués 1/89 and 6/89 & Fontrier, p.160.

28 'Mengistu has Decided to Burn Us like Wood', pp.9-11.

29 The training of this division began in mid-January 1987, and its officers and other ranks were hand-picked, with intention of creating an elite formation. However, disillusioned with the Derg, the same officers did their best to sabotage the build-up process of this unit: thus, it never reached the fighting power of the 102nd Airborne Division, see Ayele 2014, p.38.

30 People's Voice, Vol. 11/No.1.

31 Ayele 2014, p.165; Tareke 2009, pp.276-278; Fontrier, pp.160-161 & Tekeste Maleke.

32 Ironically, most Ethiopian sources describe the 4th Infantry Division as a mechanised formation, starting with this point in time. Certainly enough, being one of the four divisions originally established by the former Imperial Ethiopian Army, the 4th was more experienced and better equipped than most units established since 1977. However, considering the number of armoured vehicles reported as captured or destroyed in February 1989, the authors cannot but conclude that this formation was still far from a status of a 'mechanised' division.

33 Ayele 2014, pp.165-1970; Tareke 2009, pp.279-283; Tekeste Maleke, TPLF Military Communiqué 6/89 & 'Evil Days: 30 Years of War and Famine in Ethiopia', p.261.

34 Ayele 2014, p.170; Tareke 2009, pp.284-286; TPLF Military Communiqué 6/89.

35   Fontrier, pp.169-185; Tareke 2009, pp.285-286 & Dawit Shifaw, pp.170-181.

36   The EPDM was officially established on 21 November 1980, by former members of the EPRP, and had an almost symbiotic relationship with the TPLF, which provided it with weapons and training. By 1986, it grew to about 2,500 combatants, and began running joint operations with the TPLF. By 1989, it established at least one division. The EPDM proved very useful because the support it enjoyed among the Amhara. On the contrary, the EDORM was a small group that never counted more than few hundred. It's existence was announced only in May 1990, when it was established by a group of 17 Ethiopian Army officers captured by the TPLF. Their leader was Colonel Asamnew Bedanie, former Deputy Commander of the 17th Infantry Division. Despite its limited size, the EDORM was highly useful because it was providing military and technical expertise at the time the insurgents were in the process of expanding their regular forces. The ODPO came into being in April 1990, around a core of Oromo officers and other ranks captured during battles between the TPLF and the Ethiopian Army. Therefore, this movement corresponded to the EPRDF in so far that it attracted the support of the Oromo. Finally, the ADU, also established in 1990, foremost functioned as a link to Afar insurgent groups that refused to rally around the EPRDF.

37   S. N., interview provided on condition of anonymity, August-September 2010.

38   Cuba still had about 2,000 soldiers deployed in Ethiopia as of 1988, foremost with the aim of countering Somalia. However, Cuban Leader Fidel Castro was anxious to get these re-deployed to Angola within the context of a general build-up to leverage an accord with South Africa in regards of Namibia. Correspondingly, after being flown out to Luanda in 82 flights of Ethiopia Airlines, the last Cuban troops officially left Ethiopian on 25 September 1989.

39   Ayele 2014, p.49 & Fontrier, pp.193-194, 202-203, 221-224.

40   Ibid & 'Evil Days: 30 Years of War and Famine in Ethiopia', pp.368-369.

41   'Mengistu has Decided to Burn Us like Wood', pp.11 & 17. While the Ethiopian and Israeli governments have both denied the delivery of CBUs, a supply of about 100 was leaked to the Washington Jewish Weekly on 12 July 1990, together with the announcement that a much larger number was postponed for fear of incurring the wrath of the US government. The same report indicated that Israel was, 'probably supplying other technical support for the [Ethiopian] air force'.

42   Desperate measures of this kind had been applied already at several instances by the time, most notably during the fall of Shire.

43   The reason for this collapse was that some units – like the 27th Infantry Division and the 30th Mechanised Brigade – were not even informed about the retreat, and thus suffered unnecessary losses during delaying action, only to find their withdrawal routes cut off when finally turning around.

44   Henceforth, and for reasons explained earlier, the abbreviation EPRDF will be used instead of TPLF.

45   Numerous officers and other ranks committed suicide during the two-week long withdrawal from Woldya to Dessie, while even more troops deserted their units.

46   Ayele 2014, pp.60 & 170-171; Dawit Shifaw, pp.162, 190, 193 & 197. The 30th and the 31st Infantry Divisions were the last established by the Derg.

47   Sparta brigades were originally envisaged as 'special commando' units. However, due to their much shortened training, they were nowhere near as cohesive or as effective as the highly-respected 3rd Infantry Division.

48   Ayele 2014, pp.176-180.

49   Hughes, pp.7-9.

50   Paulos Asfaha, interview, 3 April 2018.

51   Pateman, pp.146-147; Fontrier, pp.229-230 & Los Angeles Times, 8 January 1990.

52   The Sunday Times, 18 February 1990.

53   'Mengistu has Decided to Burn Us like Wood', p.15.

54   Ayele 2014, pp.51 & 58; Tareke 2009, pp.292-297; Fontrier, pp.230 & 370; Rogers, pp.89-90.

55   Rogers, pp.89-90.

56   'Mengistu has Decided to Burn Us like Wood', p.5.

57   Ayele 2014, pp.51 & 58, 180-183; Tareke 2009, pp.292-297; Fontrier, pp.230 & 370; Rogers, pp.89-90. While names of the pilots shot down, captured or killed during this battle remain unknown, at least four EtAF pilots assigned to the 2nd Command in Asmara are known to have been killed during the war in Eritrea. They were: Colonel Tilahun Bogale (MiG-23BN pilot), Captain Desta Abiyu (MiG-23BN pilot), Captain Abraham (Mi-24 pilot), and Lieutenant Asres Zike (MiG-21 pilot). Furthermore, the following pilots are known by the location where they were shot down and killed, but not by the date: Colonel Mengistu Kassa (MiG-21 pilot), Naqfa; Major Getahun Demissie (MiG-23 pilot), Algena; Captain Tesfaye Berhane-Selassie (MiG-23BN pilot), Keren; Lietuenant Amanuel Made-Michael (MiG-23 pilot), Mendefera; Lieutenant Tekle Mariam Tilhaun (MiG-23 pilot), Algena; and Lieutenant Hailu Tilhaun (MiG-23BN pilot), Mekelle.

58   'Mengistu has Decided to Burn Us like Wood', p.4 & 'Evil Days: 30 Years of War and Famine in Ethiopia., pp.240-242.

59   'Mengistu has Decided to Burn Us like Wood', p.4.

60   Ayele 2014, pp.51 & 58, 180-183; Tareke 2009, pp.292-297; Fontrier, pp.230 & 370; Rogers, pp.89-90.

61   'Evil Days: 30 Years of War and Famine in Ethiopia', pp.245-247.

62   Ibid, pp.245-247.

63   Fontrier, pp.230-295; Connell 1997, pp.227-235; Connell 2004, pp.617-624 'Evil Days: 30 Years of War and Famine in Ethiopia', p.246.

64   Fontrier, pp.298-301, 358-371 & 'Evil Days: 30 Years of War and Famine in Ethiopia, p.249-250.

65   Paulos Asfaha, interview, 3 April 2018. Notable is that the commanders of the three EPLA brigades deployed inside Ethiopia were Omar Hassan 'Tewil', Romedan Awelyai, and Estifanos 'Bruno'. While some sources subsequently cited as many as 'several Eritrean divisions' active inside Ethiopia, it is highly unlikely that more than three, perhaps four, brigades of Eritrean insurgents – plus a few commando-detachments embedded with the OLF and the ALF – had ever operated in central and eastern Ethiopia. Ayele (2014), on pp.198-200, cites the presence of two mechanised brigades of the EPLA in Central Ethiopia as of early 1991.

66   Ayele 2014, pp.183-186 & 274.

67   Fontrier, p.234; Tareke 2009, p.301.

68   Ayele 2014, p.187.

69   According to Ayele (2015), this happened not due to incompetence, but was an act of sabotage by an officer opposed to the Derg.

70   Ayele 2014, pp.192-197 & Ayele 2015.

71   'Mengistu has Decided to Burn Us like Wood', p.2.

72 The primary reason for this reorganisation should have been Mengistu's desire to make his control of the army an easier affair.

73 Paulos Asfaha, interview, 3 April 2018.

74 Ayele 2014, pp.199-202; Tareke 2009, pp.299-305; Fontrier, pp.275, 290 & 291.

75 Ayele 2014, pp.199-202; Tareke 2009, pp.301-304; Fontrier, pp.291-293 & 302-305.

76 Ayele 2014, p.202; Tareke 2009, pp.304-305; Fontrier, pp.294, 310-316.

77 Ayele 2014, p.203; Tareke 2009, pp.307-308; Fontrier, pp.344-346, 360-365 & 372-383.

78 Divisions mentioned by authors such as Fontrier, Ayele, and Tareke were named Aurora, Alula, Aqaqi, Awash, Maqdala, Agazi, Labadar, May Day, Ma'ebal, Yakatit, Awfifi, Lab Adar, Qy Kokab, Hawzen, Samenzo and Tewodros.

79 Other high-ranking EtAF officers imprisoned by the EPRDF as of May 1991 included Brigadier-Generals Mesfin Haile (the last commander of the 2nd Command EtAF) and Teshale Zewdie (whose last post was commander of air defences of the 2nd Command), Colonels Berhanu Kebede, Berhanu Wubneh, Asmare Getahun, Nebro Tilahun, Kasaye Kifle, Girma Asfaw, Teka Mekonnen, Belte Wondimu, Desalgn Mebrate, Tigneh Wolde-Giorgis, Asrat Tekalgn, Bezabih Tilahun, and Solomon Kebede, and Lieutenant-Colonels Lema Tekalgn, Bekele Zegeye and Amnawkew Mamo.

80 Author, date and medium of publishing unknown; translation of this interview was provided by a source in Ethiopia on condition of anonymity.

81 Fontrier, pp.371-377; Pierre Dufour, 'Rapport d'Information', Ministère de la Défence, www.troupesdemarine.org, pp.120-123.

82 This sub-chapter is based on 'Home Affairs', TV interview with Major-General Tsadkan Gebretensae (Chief-of-Staff ENDF, 1991-2001), Ethiopian National TV (henceforth ENTV), 2014; Koonings, Kees & Krujit, pp.260-268 & Mulugeta Gerehiwot Berhe.

83 Mulugeta Gebrehiwot Berhe.

84 One of the instructors at the PTS in the late 1990s was Major-General Teshale Zewdie: originally imprisoned by the EPRDF after the fall of the Derg, he was released and granted permission to continue serving with the EtAF.

85 The last Chief-of-Staff of the Army under the Derg, was Major-General Mesfin Gerekal, an Eritrean. Similarly, the last Deputy Operations EtAF was Brigadier-General Mikael Birru, a Tigrayan. On the contrary, most reports about 'complete disorder' within the 'languishing' air force of the 1990s and early 2000s seem to have been released by Ethiomedia, a 'news agency' run by Abraha Belai. While a Tigrayan, Belai was a former editor of the daily 'Ethiopian Herald', published in English, which was used to spread pro-Derg propaganda in the 1980s. As an avowed enemy of the EPRDF's government, he was fired and forced into exile, before being charged with treason in absentia for 'instigating election-related violence'.

86 S. N., interview provided on condition of anonymity, August-September 2010.

87 'President Girma inaugurated the Dejen Aviation Maintenance and Engineering Complex', Ethiopian News Agency, 30 June 2004. Except for citing the graduation of 10 jet fighter pilots (including Lieutenant Haimanot Haile Mariam, the first Ethiopian female fighter pilot), the report in question précised that the DAVEC complex includes a hangar that can accommodate 18 large and medium-sized aircraft and helicopters, administration officers and the multi-purpose auditorium, and that the company wass meanwhile the backbone of the EtAF, overhauling aircraft, helicopters, and engines, and producing spare parts.

88 According to Alexander Mladenov, in 'Bulgarian Instructor Pilots in Ethiopia', Operations, Volume 1/Issue 3, Spring 2005, Ethiopia acquired 10 L-39Cs from former Czechoslovakia in 1983, 10 in 1988, and five in 1997-1998. Furthermore, in 1997-1998, it acquired up to five MiG-23BNs from Bulgaria: the latter were cannibalised for spares used to overhaul numerous Ethiopian MiG-23BNs.

89 A separate police service was established only in October 1996.

90 Hughes, pp.2-4.

91 Ibid, pp.19-20.

92 Ibid, p.24. Moreover, in the aftermath of the Badme War, the Eritrean government militarised its entire national educational system, and integrated the same into its military and security apparatus: ever since, nearly all of the students of Eritrean colleges and universities are members of the military. Overall, as sincere and upright the EPLF originally initiated its 'social revolution', more than 25 years later there can be no doubt that the result is the establishment of a militant dictatorship with centralised economy, in which the state exercises very tight control over all aspects of public life. Unsurprisingly, obtaining hard facts about the Eritrean military and security apparatus since 1991 proved rather problematic: the number of authoritative publications can be counted on the fingers of one hand.

93 Habtesion Hadgu underwent conversion training on MiG-23s in the USSR, in 1983-1984, together with Bezabih Petros.

94 'Exposed: Secrets of the 1998-2000 Air War between Ethiopia and Eritrea', Tesfa News, 4 September 2015 (in Amharic). The essence of the TV show in question was an-hour-long interview with Captain Kinde Damte, a former EtAF MiG-pilot. Notable is that Abraham Oqbgasellassie was dismissed from the EtAF following the defection of a Canberra-crew to Somalia, during the Ogaden War.

95 Retired DIA analyst (interview provided on condition of anonymity), February 2001.

96 Storaro, p.63. Serials of the four Eritrean MB.339s were ERAF-406 to -409. Notable is that, while based on a jet trainer, the MB.339C variant (and its derivatives), was developed as a lead-in trainer with significant combat capability. It was equipped with a Litton LR80 twin-gyro inertial platform, GEC Avionics 620K tactical area navigation system, an ARINC 429 databus, Kaiser Sabre head-up display and weapons aiming computer, a multi-function CRT display, a stores management system by Logic of Italy, a FIAR/Ericsson P.0702 laser rangefinder, and compatible with a wide range of air-to-air (including missiles like AIM-9 Sidewinder and R.550 Magic) and air-to-ground weapons (including guided missiles and bombs).

97 Ibid; Cooper et al, African MiGs, Volume 1, pp.147-149 & Hughes, pp.19-24. Ironically, the instructor for the Eritrean female cadet in Ethiopia was Bezabih Petros, who spent the period 1984-1991 as prisoner of war of the EPLF/EPLA, but then re-joined the EtAF.

98 Jon Abbink, 'Badme and the Ethio-Eritrean Border: The Challenge of Demarcation in the Post-War Period', Africa: rivista trimestrale die studi e documentazione, pp.219-231.

99 Sean D Murphy, The Eritrean-Ethiopian War (1998-2000), George Washington University Law School, 2016, p.2.

100 Ibid, p.2.

101 Ibid, p.4-5.

102 'Home Affairs', TV interview with Major-General Tsadkan Gebretensae, ENTV, 2014.

103 'Eritrea's Preparations for War in March 1998', VOA, 15 June 1998.

104 Hughes, pp.25-27.

105 Although its designation remains unknown, Ethiopian sources interviewed on condition of anonymity stress that the brigade in question was largely staffed by troops educated at the EPLF-run school Biet Tmhrti Sewra, in Naqfa, for children orphaned by the war of the 1970s and 1980s. The school had a reputation for producing rough and though kids of extraordinary discipline, named 'fitewaris', that spoke not a single word of Amharic (which used to be compulsory in all of Ethiopia, and thus in most of Eritrea before 1991). Most new ERAF pilots trained in the mid-1990s were educated at the same school.

106 According to contemporary news on the ETNV, further decisions of the Ethiopian government included precautionary measures with respect to Eritreans on its soil. For example, all the ERAF cadets undergoing training in Ethiopia were detained; all the males of military age suspected of posing a threat to national security – on account of their military training, for example – were detained and imprisoned at temporary camps, with full access of the ICRC (according to its release from 10 July 1998, the ICRC confirmed to have visited the 'prisoner of war camp' at Fiche on 20, 26, and 27 June, and on 2 July that year). Functionaries of the EPLF's offices in Addis Ababa were expelled from the country, while their families were given the choice of remaining in Ethiopia if they wanted to do so. Finally, any Eritreans caught while engaged in 'intelligence-gathering activities' or 'collecting financial or other resources', were arrested and expelled.

107 On 24 May 1991, the ENTV forwarded a statement issued by the government in Addis Ababa, according to which the Ethiopian troops removed 30,375 anti-personnel and 539 anti-tank mines in the Badme area alone.

108 UNHC release, 17 December 1998. According to the same report, the Eritrean government expelled over 39,000 Ethiopians from the country by December 1998.

109 S. N., interview provided on condition of anonymity, August-September 2010 & 'Exposed: Secrets of the 1998-2000 Air War between Ethiopia and Eritrea', Tesfa News, 4 September 2015 (in Amharic).

110 UN, Reports of International Arbitral Awards, Eritrea-Ethiopia Claims Commission – Partial Award: Central Front – Ethiopia's Claim 2, 28 April 2004, pp.187-190. The UN commission concluded that there is no credible evidence that Eritrea intentionally targeted Ethiopian civilians. Instead, it leaned towards inexperienced Eritrean pilots making a mistake, or releasing their ordnance much too early when confronted with anti-aircraft fire from Ethiopian air defences. Furthermore the UN commission found no credible evidence for Ethiopian claims that on the same day the ERAF also bombed Axum and Adigrat.

111 S. N., interview provided on condition of anonymity, August-September 2010 & 'Exposed: Secrets of the 1998-2000 Air War between Ethiopia and Eritrea', Tesfa News, 4 September 2015 (in Amharic).

112 According to contemporary reports in the Eritrean media, Petros flew the MiG-21bis with serial number '1083' during that mission.

113 UN, Reports of International Arbitral Awards, Eritrea-Ethiopia Claims Commission – Partial Award: Central Front – Ethiopia's Claim 2, 28 April 2004, pp.187-190. The UN commission concluded that there is no credible evidence that Eritrea intentionally targeted Ethiopian civilians on this occasion, nor definite confirmation that the damage was actually caused by an air strike flown by the ERAF.

114 UN, Reports of International Arbitral Awards, Eritrea-Ethiopia Claims Commission – Partial Award: Western Front, Aerial Bombardment and Related Claims – Eritrea's Claims, 1, 3, 5, 9-13, 14, 21, 25 & 26, 17 December 2004, pp.314-315.

115 'Dejen Ande Hishel: The Prison Breaker', Assenna.com, 27 February 2014 (in Tigrinya).

116 Ibid. According to the same interview, reports along which two MiG-29s were written off following a collision on take-off from Asmara, early after their delivery, were not correct. The ERAF did lose two MiG-29s during the Badme War, and had another one badly damaged, but the first crash of a MiG-29 in Eritrea occurred only in 2004.

117 The 1998-99 World Defence Almanac, Military Technology (magazine), Volume XXIII, Issue 1, 1999, p.241 & 'Home Affairs', TV interview with Major-General Tsadkan Gebretensae, ENTV, 2014.

118 Dr. Aleksander Andreevich Raspletin, History PVO website (historykpvo.narod2.ru), 2013 & Ethiopia: The Mengistu Regime and Its Relations With Moscow', CIA, ALA 84-10084X, August 1984, CIA/FOIA/ER.

119 Furthermore, by 2002, the Ethiopians imported at least one Ukrainian-made Kolchuga electronic support measures systems, designed to detect and track aircraft by triangulation and multilateration of radio frequencies of their emissions.

120 A. I., 'African Fighter Aircraft and the Problems of Russia', AviaPort.ru, 27 March 2009.

121 Reportedly 'Soviet Jews', all the pilots in question spoke Russian only, and thus next to nothing is known about their subsequent experiences in Ethiopia. Another loss the EtAF suffered during this period included an Mi-8 helicopter that crashed near Koka River, in September 1998, killing the crew of three, including Captain Tsegaye, a senior technician named Abraham Shino (both used to serve with the EtAF before 1991), and a Russian instructor.

122 Alexander Mladenov, 'Bulgarian Instructor Pilots in Ethiopia', Operations, Volume 1/Issue 3, Spring 2005.

123 Ibid. In comparison, Ethiopian sources (interviewed on condition of anonymity) stress that the seven students trained by the Bulgarians never completed their training, but had to be re-qualified by Ethiopian instructors once the Bulgarians were requested to leave.

124 Although variants designated R-27ER and R-27ET, equipped with bigger motors for extended range, are in widespread service in Russia and around the world, the suffix 'E' in the case of R-27ERs and R-27ETs delivered to Ethiopia in late 1998 is said to have meant 'export'. Accordingly, the missiles in question have had a narrower and shorter engagement envelope (maximum of 50 kilometres/32 nautical miles in head-on mode, and less than 20 kilometres/12.4 miles in pursuit mode), and no capability to be fired without a radar lock-on.

125 S. N., interview provided on condition of anonymity, February 2018 & A. I., 'African Fighter Aircraft and the Problems of Russia'. Claims by unofficial Russian sources, according to whom the first Ethiopian converted to Su-27s was nobody less than the Chief-of-Staff EtAF, Major-General Abebe Tekle Haimanot, are unrealistic. There is no doubt that he was offered a few 'guided tours' of the aircraft, though.

126 Ibid.

127 Mladenov, 'Bulgarian Instructor Pilots in Ethiopia' & A. I., 'African Fighter Aircraft and the Problems of Russia'.

128 A. I., 'African Fighter Aircraft and the Problems of Russia'. On the contrary, Ethiopian sources stress the four pilots provided by the Danubian only helped establish a helicopter test-pilot school, related to the DAVEC.

129 The arrival of Su-27s at Mekelle, together with the group of Russian ground personnel, prompted countless reports with titles like 'Russians Fly for both Sides in Horn of Africa (The Times, 19 February 1999). However, all available Ethiopian sources deny that any Russian pilots present in Ethiopia as of 1999 had ever flown any combat sorties.

130 S. N., interview provided on condition of anonymity, December 2008, August-September 2010 & February 2018.

131 'News', ENTV, 10 February 1999. In the course of the show in question, the Ethiopian TV crew ran interviews with Lieutenant Alemayehu Getachew (MiG-21 pilot), and Lieutenant Mulugeta Wolde-Rufael (MiG-23 pilot). Transcriptions from the same interview were published in the state-owned magazine Efoyta, in March 1999.

132 Retired DIA analyst (interview provided on condition of anonymity), February 2001; Mladenov, 'Bulgarian Instructor Pilots in Ethiopia', & A. I., 'African Fighter Aircraft and the Problems of Russia'.

133 'Home Affairs', TV interview with Major-General Tsadkan Gebretensae, ENTV, 2014.

134 A. I., 'African Fighter Aircraft and the Problems of Russia', AviaPort.ru.

135 From what is known about ERAF losses during this war, the damaged aircraft was the sole Eritrean MiG-29UB, serial number ERAF 501.

136 'Home Affairs', TV interview with Major-General Tsadkan Gebretensae, ENTV, 2014.

137 UN, Reports of International Arbitral Awards, Eritrea-Ethiopia Claims Commission – Partial Award: Western and Eastern Fronts – Ethiopia's Claims 1 & 3, 19 December 2005, p.364.

138 The final scene of this clash was captured by a team of the ENTV, resulting in one of most famous videos of the Badme War.

139 'Dejen Ande Hishel: The Prison Breaker', Assenna.com, 27 February 2014.

140 Retired DIA analyst (interview provided on condition of anonymity), February 2001 & A. I., 'African Fighter Aircraft and the Problems of Russia'.

141 'Dejen Ande Hishel: The Prison Breaker', Assenna.com, 27 February 2014. Brigadier-General Hadgu's fate was remarkably similar. In 2003, he was dismissed and jailed following defection of five Eritrean pilots sent for training in Ukraine. His replacement as the Chief-of-Staff ERAF, Major-General Teklay Habte-Selassie, was a relatively experienced officer that used to command the Sawa Training Centre, and then served a tour as administrative chief of Asseb. However, he obviously lacked any kind of qualifications related to the air force and was almost certainly appointed for his loyalty to President Afewerki, instead for his expertise in regards of air power.

142 'Eritrea captured Ethiopian Helicopter', Visafric.com, 19 March 1999.

143 'Dejen Ande Hishel: The Prison Breaker', Assenna.com, 27 February 2014 & Alex Last, 'Hundreds killed in the Horn', BBC, 16 March 1999. According to Last, he counted more than 300 killed Ethiopians and about 20 destroyed tanks after the clash of 15 March 1999.

144 'Eritrea accepts Peace Deal after Ethiopian Incursion', CNN, 27 February 1999; 'Ethiopia declares Victory', BBC, 1 March 1999; 'Ethiopian-Eritrean War of Words continues', BBC, 15 July 1999; Mariam Demassie Laeke, 'Touring the Ethiopian Front', BBC, 23 July 1999.

145 Mideksa and Bekele are known to have both served with the EtAF already before 1991.

146 Indeed, according to a retired DIA analyst (interview provided on condition of anonymity, February 2001) Asmara failed to successfully conclude even negotiations for a batch of about 50 extended-range R-27ET air-to-air missiles with Ukraine, run during the second half of 1999.

147 Abayneh was from Addis Zemen in Gondar, and joined the EtAF as a cadet in mid-1990s. Notable is that on 29 August 1999, a mishap related to No. 6 Squadron resulted in Ethiopian air defences learning an important lesson about the need to maintain a credible interceptor force. The affair in question began with early warning radars at Mekelle detecting the appearance of an unknown aircraft over Asmara and underway in southern direction. Because it took seven minutes to tow one of the Su-27SKs from the apron to the start of the runway, its scramble was cancelled and the air defences of the forward Ethiopian air base were ordered into action. Several SA-2 and SA-3 SAMs were fired, one of which shot down the unknown aircraft – a privately owned Learjet 35A, registration N350JF, operated by the company Corporate Jets on a flight from Naples, via Luxor and Nairobi to Lanseria, in South Africa. Although the crew intended to follow a route from Asmara to Djibouti, for unknown reasons it strayed off its course and ended deep inside the no-fly zone over northern Ethiopia. Both civilians on board were killed before the wreckage of their aircraft hit the ground, about 30 kilometres north of Adwa.

148 UN, Reports of International Arbitral Awards', Eritrea-Ethiopia Claims Commission – Partial Award: Western Front, Aerial Bombardment and Related Claims – Eritrea's Claims, 1, 3, 5, 9-13, 14, 21, 25 & 26', 17 December 2004, pp.306, 314-315.

149 That said, the EtAF is known to have lost a MiG-23BN during a training flight from Bahir Dar AB, in August 2000. The pilot ejected safely.

150 UN, Reports of International Arbitral Awards, Eritrea-Ethiopia Claims Commission – Partial Award: Central Front – Ethiopia's Claim 2, 28 April 2004, p307.

151 Ibid, p.333. Faced with Eritrean accusations that this attack represented an act of a 'war crime', Ethiopia subsequently maintained that the power plant was not the original objective, but that its MiG-23BNs intended to target the port of Massawa. As they approached the area, the fighter-bombers may have been fired upon by the Eritrean SAM-site protecting the power plant. Their pilots then requested permission to switch targets and attacked the SAM-site in question. In return, Eritrea claimed that the aircraft flew so low, that they were detected only shortly before releasing their ordnance, and that the attack on the power plant was thus intentional (see 'Reports of International Arbitral Awards'). The UN commission concluded that either way this attack did not constitute a war crime.

152 'Horn Peace Deal: Full Text', BBC, 11 December 2000.

153 'Ruling: Eritrea broke International Law in Ethiopia Attack', CNN, 21 December 2005.